BATTLE FOR
ST-LÔ

The 'Battle Zone Normandy' Series

Orne Bridgehead Lloyd Clark

Sword Beach Ken Ford

Juno Beach Ken Ford

Gold Beach Simon Trew

Omaha Beach Stephen Badsey & Tim Bean

Utah Beach Stephen Badsey

Villers-Bocage George Forty

Battle for Cherbourg R.P.W. Havers

Operation Epsom Lloyd Clark

Battle for St-Lô Peter Yates

Battle for Caen Simon Trew & Stephen Badsey

Operation Cobra Christopher Pugsley

Road to Falaise Stephen Hart

Falaise Pocket Paul Latawski

All of these titles can be ordered via the
Sutton Publishing website
www.suttonpublishing.co.uk

**The 'Battle Zone Normandy'
Editorial and Design Team**

Series Editor Simon Trew

Senior Commissioning Editor Jonathan Falconer

Assistant Editor Nick Reynolds

Cover and Page Design Martin Latham

Editing and Layout Donald Sommerville

Mapping Map Creation Ltd

Photograph Scanning and Mapping Bow Watkinson

Index Michael Forder

BATTLE ZONE NORMANDY

BATTLE FOR ST-LÔ

PETER YATES

Series Editor: Simon Trew

Sutton Publishing

First Published in 2004 by
Sutton Publishing Limited · Phoenix Mill
Thrupp · Stroud · Gloucestershire · GL5 2BU

Text Copyright © Peter Yates 2004
Tour map overlays Copyright © Sutton
  Publishing
Tour base maps Copyright © Institut
  Géographique National, Paris
GSGS (1944) map overlays Copyright ©
  Sutton Publishing
GSGS (1944) base maps Copyright ©
  The British Library/Crown Copyright

Peter Yates has asserted the moral right to be
identified as the author of this work.

British Library Cataloguing in Publication Data
A catalogue record for this book is available
from The British Library.

ISBN 0-7509-3018-7

While every effort has been made to ensure
that the information given in this book is
accurate, the publishers, the author and the
series editor do not accept responsibility for
any errors or omissions or for any changes in
the details given in this guide or for the
consequence of any reliance on the
information provided. The publishers would be
grateful if readers would advise them of any
inaccuracies they may encounter so these can
be considered for future editions of this book.
The inclusion of any place to stay, place to eat,
tourist attraction or other establishment in
this book does not imply an endorsement or
recommendation by the publisher, the series
editor or the author. Their details are included
for information only. Directions are for
guidance only and should be used in
conjunction with other sources of information.

Typeset in 10.5/14 pt Sabon

Printed and bound in England by
J.H. Haynes & Co. Ltd, Sparkford

Front cover: US artillery supports First US Army's offensive, 11 July 1944. *(United States National Archives [USNA])*

Page 1: The memorial to civilian victims of the war in the Place Charles de Gaulle, St-Lô. *(Author)*

Page 3: A foot patrol in St-Lô. The tower of Notre-Dame cathedral, visible in the distance, was used by US artillery observers after the town's capture to spot targets to the south. *(USNA)*

Page 7: A Stuart light tank in the streets of St-Lô, 20 July. Note the use of sandbags to give extra protection to the tank. *(USNA)*

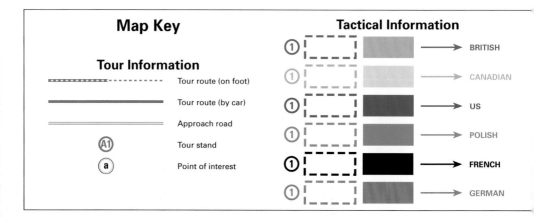

Map Key

Tour Information

···············	Tour route (on foot)
───────────	Tour route (by car)
═══════════	Approach road
(A1)	Tour stand
(a)	Point of interest

Tactical Information

①	▭ (dashed)	──▶ BRITISH
①	▭ (dashed)	──▶ CANADIAN
①	▭ (dashed)	──▶ US
①	▭ (dashed)	──▶ POLISH
①	▭ (dashed)	──▶ FRENCH
①	▭ (dashed)	──▶ GERMAN

CONTENTS

THE NORMANDY BATTLEFIELD

● Town
  Railway
  Road
▬▬▬ Caen Canal
▬ ▬ ▬ Département boundary

Contour 100 metres
Contour 200 metres
Contour 300 metres

0   25   50
Kilometres

Bay of the Seine

Cherbourg

Valognes   Quineville
            Montebourg
Ste. Mère Eglise   UTAH
Barneville   OMAHA   Port en Bessin   Arromanches   Courseulles   Le Havre
        R. Douve   St. Laurent   GOLD   JUNO
        R. Aure   SWORD
Carentan   Isigny   Ouistreham   Cabourg
        R. Taute   Bayeux   Houlgate
Lessay   R. Seulles
Périers   R. Drôme
        MANCHE   St. Lô   Caumont   R. Odon   Caen   Argences   Lisie
Coutances   R. Vire   Villers-Bocage   Mézidon
                                                    CALVADOS   R. Dives
                                                            Falaise
Granville   Condé   R. Orne
                Vire   Argentan
        Avranches   Flers   ORNE
        Mortain   R. Sélune
                        Domfront
                R. Mayenne
        Fougères   Alençon

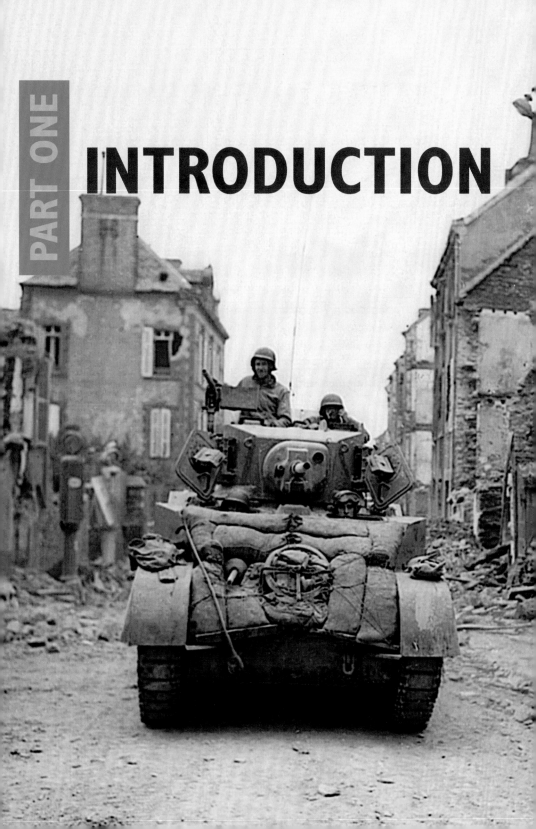

PART ONE

INTRODUCTION

BATTLE ZONE NORMANDY

The Battle of Normandy was one of the greatest military clashes of all time. From late 1943, when the Allies appointed their senior commanders and began the air operations that were such a vital preliminary to the invasion, until the end of August 1944, it pitted against one another several of the most powerful nations on earth, as well as some of their most brilliant minds. When it was won, it changed the world forever. The price was high, but for anybody who values the principles of freedom and democracy, it is difficult to conclude that it was one not worth paying.

I first visited Lower Normandy in 1994, a year after I joined the War Studies Department at the Royal Military Academy Sandhurst (RMAS). With the 50th anniversary of D-Day looming, it was decided that the British Army would be represented at several major ceremonies by one of the RMAS's officer cadet companies. It was also suggested that the cadets should visit some of the battlefields, not least to bring home to them the significance of why they were there. Thus, at the start of June 1994, I found myself as one of a small team of military and civilian directing staff flying with the cadets in a draughty and noisy Hercules transport to visit the beaches and fields of Calvados, in my case for the first time.

I was hooked. Having met some of the veterans and seen the ground over which they fought – and where many of their friends died – I was determined to go back. Fortunately, the Army encourages battlefield touring as part of its soldiers' education, and on numerous occasions since 1994 I have been privileged to return to Normandy, often to visit new sites. In the process I have learned a vast amount, both from my colleagues (several of whom are contributors to this series) and from my enthusiastic and sometimes tri-service audiences, whose professional insights and penetrating questions have frequently made me re-examine my own assumptions and prejudices. Perhaps inevitably, especially when standing in one of Normandy's beautifully-maintained Commonwealth War Graves Commission cemeteries, I have also found myself deeply moved by the critical events that took place there in the summer of 1944.

'Battle Zone Normandy' was conceived by Jonathan Falconer, Commissioning Editor at Sutton Publishing, in 2001. Why not, he suggested, bring together recent academic research – some of which challenges the general perception of what happened on and after 6 June 1944 – with a perspective based on familiarity with the ground itself? We agreed that the opportunity existed for a series that would set out to combine detailed and accurate narratives, based mostly on primary sources, with illustrated guides to the ground itself, which could be used either in the field (sometimes quite literally), or by the armchair explorer. The book in your hands is the product of that agreement.

The 'Battle Zone Normandy' series consists of 14 volumes, covering most of the major and many of the minor engagements that went together to create the Battle of Normandy. The first six books deal with the airborne and amphibious landings on 6 June 1944, and with the struggle to create the firm lodgement that was the prerequisite for eventual Allied victory. Five further volumes cover some of the critical battles that followed, as the Allies' plans unravelled and they were forced to improvise a battle very different from that originally intended. Finally, the last three titles in the series examine the fruits of the bitter attritional struggle of June and July 1944, as the Allies irrupted through the German lines or drove them back in fierce fighting. The series ends, logically enough, with the devastation of the German armed forces in the 'Falaise Pocket' in late August.

Whether you use these books while visiting Normandy, or to experience the battlefields vicariously, we hope you will find them as interesting to read as we did to research and write. Far from the inevitable victory that is sometimes represented, D-Day and the ensuing battles were full of hazards and unpredictability. Contrary to the view often expressed, had the invasion failed, it is far from certain that a second attempt could have been mounted. Remember this, and the significance of the contents of this book, not least for your life today, will be the more obvious.

Dr Simon Trew
Royal Military Academy Sandhurst
December 2003

THE NORMANDY BATTLEFIELD, MID-JUNE TO MID-JULY

Legend:
- Allied front line, evening 12 June
- Contour 50 metres
- Contour 100 metres
- Contour 200 metres
- Inundated area

Kilometres 0 10 20

CAP DE LA HAGUE

POINTE DE BARFLEUR

CAP LÉVI

Auderville
Beaumont-Hague
CHERBOURG
St-Pierre-Église
Barfleur
Tourlaville
Delasse
Quettehou
St-Vaast-la-Hougue
Quinéville
VALOGNES
Montebourg
R. Merderet
Bricquebec
Orglandes
Ste-Mère-Église
Chef-du-Pont
Pont-l'Abbé
St-Sauveur-le-Vicomte
Barneville
St-Lô-d'Ourville
la Haye-du-Puits
R. Douve
les Pieux

CAP DE FLAMANVILLE
CAP DE CARTERET

Bay of the Seine

Lessay
Périers
St-Sauveur-Lendelin
COUTANCES
Marigny
Condé-sur-Vire
ST-LÔ
R. Taute
R. Vire
Pont-Hébert
St-Jean-de-Daye
Montmartin-en-Graignes
Carentan
Isigny
Grandcamp-les-Bains
Vierville-sur-Mer
Port-en-Bessin
Arromanches-les-Bains
R. Aure
R. Drôme
le Molay-Littry
Trungy
Balleroy
Villiers-Fossard
St-Clair-sur-l'Elle
Bérigny
Hottot-les-Bagues
Caumont
Noyers-Bocage
Villers-Bocage
Tilly-sur-Seulles
BAYEUX
Courseulles-sur-Mer
R. Seulles
Carpiquet
St-Manvieu
Cambes
Lion-sur-Mer
Ouistreham
R. Orne
CAEN
CABOURG
R. Dives
Hérouvillette
Troarn
Cagny
Vimont
May-sur-Orne
Évrecy
R. Odon

BESSIN
BOCAGE

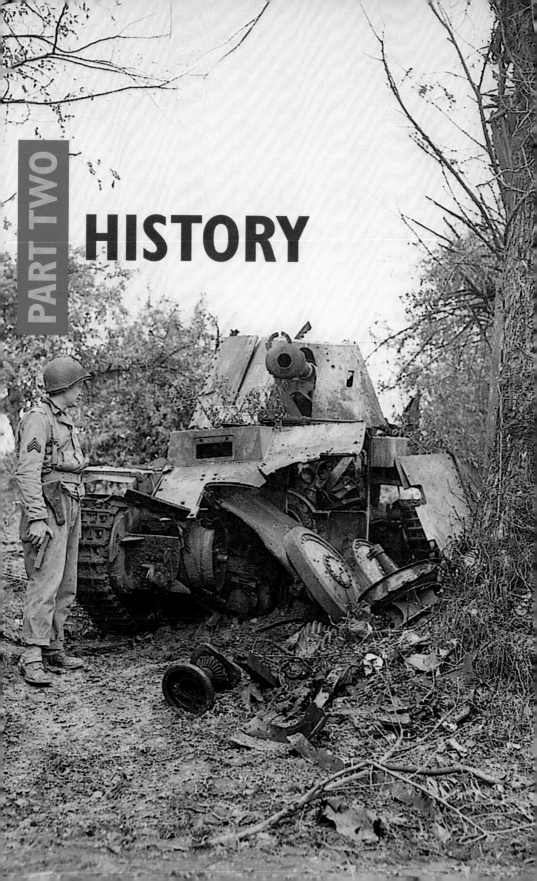

PART TWO

HISTORY

CHAPTER I

THE PHYSICAL AND STRATEGIC CONTEXT

St-Lô is a country town of medium size, capital of the *département* of the Manche, home of France's national stud with a weekly general market. Medieval walls surround the old centre, on an outcrop of rock. But there are few old buildings apart from some preserved ruins. These are evidence of the destruction of the town in 1944.

THE BATTLE AREA

Geography made St-Lô an important military objective. The town was at the centre of road and railway communications in western Normandy, with a population in 1944 of 11,000. It was also the site of two bridges over the River Vire, which runs northwards to enter the sea 26 kilometres (km) from the town. Telephone and telegraph wires converged on St-Lô from all directions. To the east the country is a mass of low hills and ridges, most running east–west, cut by small creeks running through steep valleys. North-west of the town the grain of the country runs north to south, parallel with the Vire, until it gives way to the Carentan marshes about 15 km away. South-west of St-Lô the terrain is more open, with a road net more suitable for rapid movement by large numbers of vehicles.

The Vire between St-Lô and the sea was 13–20 metres wide, deep and fast. North of the town, there were bridges at Pont-Hébert, St-Fromond, la Raye and Isigny-sur-Mer. For some distance north-west of St-Lô the Terrette runs roughly parallel to the Vire, 2–4 km away, before diverging to join the Taute, which flows parallel with the Vire for 10 km south of Carentan. The Terrette was a smaller waterway than the Vire or Taute, but still an effective constraint on movement. About 13 km north of St-Lô, the Vire–Taute Canal cuts north-west from the Vire through wetlands and spurs of higher ground. In 1944 it offered an obvious barrier, either against US

Above: The ruined prize. Jeeps approaching St-Lô from the north after the capture of the town. *(USNA)*

Page 11: A knocked out Marder III, possibly from German 352nd Infantry Division's anti-tank battalion. The Marder III's 76-mm gun was used for a variety of fire support tasks. Its open-topped crew compartment made it vulnerable to grenades and mortar rounds, both widely used in the *bocage*. *(USNA)*

troops advancing inland or against German forces counter-attacking towards the coast. The River Aure flows westwards, parallel with the coast, to join the Vire at Isigny. Near Trévières the Aure is fed by a tributary, the Tortonne. Between this river junction and Isigny, 12 km away, the Aure's course is bordered by water meadows, some 2 km wide in 1944. This obstacle is 22 km north of St-Lô and 4–7 km south from Omaha Beach. Halfway from the Aure to St-Lô the Elle runs north-westerly to join the Vire; a mere creek, but with steep and cluttered banks that made it a significant obstacle. About 15 km east of St-Lô the Drôme, running south to north, marked the boundary in June 1944 between the First US Army area to the west and Second (British) Army to the east. It was also the eastern limit of the German Seventh Army in the period covered by this book.

In addition to the natural water barriers German engineers had contrived to flood areas of western Normandy, in particular blocking the drainage sluices to make the Carentan marshes and Aure water meadows broader and wetter.

View south-east along the River Vire from the bridge at St-Fromond. On 7 July, elements of US 3rd Armored Division crossed this bridge after it was repaired by American engineers. *(Author)*

High ground was critical in the fighting. St-Lô lies in a saucer and is itself indefensible. Heights to the north and east were therefore essential to the defence of the town. In 1944 these appeared on the belligerents' maps with contours and spot heights based on old and unreliable surveys. This was a problem for the soldiers, who found that possession of a particular grid reference did not necessarily put them in the dominating position that they expected. Present-day visitors using accurate modern maps can therefore have difficulty locating some of the most important terrain features of 1944. Since they played such a critical role in the fighting, however, it is worth recording the position of some of them here.

Dominating St-Lô from the north was Hill 122, which rose above the suburb of St-Georges-Montcoq. On US maps the hilltop was just west of the D191 road, which links St-Lô with the village of Villiers-Fossard; in fact, the highest part of this feature (138 metres above sea level) was 1 km further east, next to the D6 highway. East of St-Lô the most significant feature was the Martinville Ridge, which ascends to 155 metres near St-André-de-l'Épine, about 6 km north-east of St-Lô. From here the ground continues to rise to its highest point at Hill 192, 1.5 km east of St-André-de-l'Épine. This piece of terrain was regarded by both sides as the best observation post in the area, and was heavily fought over. One kilometre west of Pont-Hébert, heights at les Hauts Vents (Point 91 on 1944 maps, although only 73 metres on modern maps) provided magnificent views of the surrounding countryside. Various minor features were also useful as outposts and supports: an unobtrusive nose of ground at le Carillon, 2.5 km east of Pont-Hébert, covered routes south to St-Lô; high ground near Villiers-Fossard (Hill 108) and another feature at le Cauchais (on the opposite side of the D6 from Hill 122) guarded the Martinville Ridge. South of the ridge, near la Barre-de-Semilly, Hill 101 was an excellent base for fire support to troops emplaced there; the Bois du Soulaire, on the eastern slopes of Hill 192, sheltered the rear echelons of German troops on that height.

The view from the south side of the Vire–Taute Canal, looking south along the N174 highway. This long, straight road was regarded by the Germans as one of the most likely avenues for an attack against St-Lô. (Author)

There were no other substantial towns in the St-Lô sector. Small towns and villages along the rivers and major roads did have some military significance but the country was, and is, primarily dedicated to farming, with the population living in small villages and hamlets. These places were connected by a dense network of lanes and tracks, many of them sunk down between high banks. They twist and turn so as to confuse the unfamiliar traveller; it is still easy to get lost. A number of major roads were useful. The highway from St-Lô via Pont-Hébert to Carentan ('Highway 2' in US accounts; now the N174) was a vital axis for offensive operations. The D11/D6, running parallel with the Vire on its east bank between Isigny and

St-Lô, was similarly valuable. The D972/D572 connecting St-Lô to Bayeux provided lateral communication and an avenue of attack. The D900 from St-Lô to Périers, the main lateral route for the Germans west of the Vire, was another important objective for US attacks. (Throughout this account roads are identified by the numbers shown on the modern maps most readily available to readers, though these numbers may not have been in use in 1944.)

In a typical sunken lane, a jeep has passed, but only just. Meanwhile, signallers have laid telephone wire along the gully bank. The photo was taken east of St-Lô on 13 July. *(USNA)*

Roads were the only convenient way to cross the marshes. They were also the best way of getting through the *bocage* countryside that covered the rest of the sector. From above, *bocage* resembled a rumpled patchwork quilt, worked mostly in green. The ground was divided up into irregular pastures, orchards and woods by tall solid hedgerows – broad banks of compacted soil, bound by the roots of bushes and trees, impervious to small arms fire and resilient in the face of artillery and high explosive. The sunken lanes gave routes for concealed movement; farm buildings – many with deep cellars – provided strongpoints. Every hedgerow threatened a short-range ambush and obstructed movement, and lines of sight. American soldiers on the ground perceived the *bocage* as a lethal maze that inflicted a demoralising combination of uncertainty and danger on all who stayed too long. They called it the 'Green Hell'.

Weather also affected operations. The maritime climate of Normandy is mild, but brings frequent changes of weather and there are often days of mist and rain in summer. Cloud and mist inhibited the use of aircraft and reduced the effectiveness of artillery. Rain fed the swamps and rivers, making movement difficult and life in the field more wretched. There was also a severe storm on 19–21 June, which had a strategic impact. The American 'Mulberry' harbour (one of two artificial ports built off the beaches to support the Allied build-up in Normandy) was wrecked and Allied shipping was damaged. After this troops and supplies for First US Army arrived more slowly for a time, which restricted levels of activity.

THE OPPOSING SIDES

American commanders were aware of the value of St-Lô from well before D-Day. The original plan for the invasion emphasised the necessity of seizing Cherbourg, the important port at the top of the Cotentin peninsula, but also demanded an advance south-west to take harbours in Brittany. St-Lô was recognised as an important German headquarters, a communications centre, and a choke-point on the routes that would be used by German forces moving to the invasion area. Accordingly, the town was bombed to impede the passage of troops. The plan as of 6 June 1944 demanded the capture of the town on 15 June to facilitate exploitation to the south-west. As usual, however, the plan was distorted by military reality.

US forces in the battle for St-Lô came under the control of Lieutenant General (Lt Gen) Omar N. Bradley, commander of First US Army. His priority in the opening stages of the invasion was to secure and connect the landing beaches. This would necessitate an advance south from Omaha Beach by Major General (Maj Gen) Leonard T. Gerow's V US Corps, to cross the Aure and Tortonne

Rivers and to defeat any counter-attacks. Connecting Omaha with Utah Beach, on the south-east side of the Cotentin peninsula, would require US forces to secure the area between Isigny and Carentan. This would involve Maj Gen J. Lawton Collins' VII US Corps, a mix of airborne and amphibiously-landed forces. Particular attention was to be paid to the area between the Vire and Taute Rivers, where an advance south to the Vire–Taute Canal would provide security in depth. Meanwhile, V Corps' 29th Infantry Division was to attack south towards the River Elle and the high ground near St-Lô, with 1st and 2nd Infantry Divisions filling the gap between it and Second (British) Army to the east. If all went well, St-Lô would fall before the Germans could reinforce the area, avoiding a difficult urban battle or an attritional slog through the *bocage*.

(*From left*) Lt Gen Omar Bradley, commanding First US Army; Maj Gen Leonard T. Gerow, commanding V US Corps; General Dwight D. Eisenhower, Supreme Allied Commander; and Maj Gen James Lawton Collins, commanding VII US Corps. (*USNA*)

In the event, V Corps proved unable to capture St-Lô by the date envisaged, or for a month afterwards. By early July the American forces committed to the battle had increased substantially. By then, in addition to V Corps, Maj Gen Charles Corlett's XIX US Corps had entered the line. A portion of Collins' VII Corps also became directly involved in the struggle for St-Lô, while forces further afield – notably Maj Gen Troy Middleton's VIII US Corps – had an

A 105-mm gun fires from a pit covered by a camouflage net, with a field telephone installed on the right. The intimate co-operation between infantry battalions and their supporting artillery was vital to American success in the battle for St-Lô. *(USNA)*

important indirect influence on the battle. For various reasons, St-Lô became a critical point to the American and German armies that could not be by-passed. These factors caused a series of bloody engagements that ended with the capture of the ruined town on 18 July. One week later the US break-out – Operation 'Cobra' – began, sustained by troops and supplies passing through St-Lô.

Facing the Americans in the battle for St-Lô was part of the German Army Group B, commanded until 17 July – when he was wounded – by *Generalfeldmarschall* (Field Marshal) Erwin Rommel. Rommel was himself subordinate to the Commander-in-Chief West (OB West), Field Marshal Gerd von Rundstedt (who was sacked and replaced by Field Marshal Günther von Kluge on 2 July). In Lower Normandy itself, resistance was organised by Seventh Army, at first under *Generalleutnant* (GenLt) Friedrich Dollmann, and then, after Dollmann committed suicide on 28 June, by *SS-Oberstgruppenführer* (General) Paul Hausser. The opposition encountered by US First Army in the early stages of the struggle for St-Lô came from Seventh Army's LXXXIV Corps, with its headquarters in the town. On D-Day, LXXXIV Corps was responsible for the entire invasion sector. However, as reinforcements arrived, it relinquished control of the area east of the Vire to II Paratroop Corps and other forces. (A list of major units used by the Germans in the battle can be found on pp. 22–3.)

A 152-mm artillery piece taken from the Russians, then used by the Germans until captured again by the Americans. The use of foreign weapons gave the Germans additional firepower, but seriously complicated their supply arrangements. (USNA)

Following the Allies' successful landings, German commanders believed that their enemies' general intent was to make a major offensive southwards between Caen and Bayeux, from British (Second) Army's sector. In this regard they became acutely anxious about the 'Caumont Gap', an area east of St-Lô between Balleroy and Bayeux which initially was almost undefended. St-Lô was an important point on the route of some reinforcements, arriving from Brittany, ordered for a while to fill this gap or join in a more ambitious scheme for a counter-attack to recapture Bayeux. In the western sector, the Germans believed that First US Army would prioritise securing the beachhead and capturing Cherbourg. These assumptions were confirmed by study of captured documents taken in the first few days of the invasion.

Although the commanders in theatre were aware of their limitations, Hitler and his staff forced them to adopt a strategy that was more offensive and optimistic than they wished. In particular, Hitler demanded the annihilation of the Allies, sector by sector, starting in the east. In the meantime German Seventh Army, facing Bradley's forces, was to make a local attack to take control of the area between Isigny and Carentan, to keep the Omaha and Utah beachheads separate and hold firm in the Cotentin and elsewhere.

These attacks failed completely. By 9 June the Germans had lost the initiative, and were never to regain it at the strategic level. On 17 June von Rundstedt and Rommel tried to explain the true situation to Hitler himself, at a conference in northern France. They said that Normandy was the Allies' major invasion area, which must be contained with massive reinforcement from other places. They explained that, in the face of Allied ground forces with powerful air and naval support, the beachheads could not be eliminated. Allied intentions were to make a major break-out from the Caen–Bayeux area, with a secondary offensive from the US sector to seize the ports in Brittany. Without radical steps, the Allies were bound to succeed. Cherbourg would fall, then Caen and St-Lô. According to Rommel the only chance of strategic success was to withdraw east of the Orne, hold the river with infantry, assemble a grand mobile reserve and attack westwards into the American sector, driving into the flank of the Cotentin.

Hitler was not moved by the appreciation or the plan. He believed the Allies would land a larger invasion force elsewhere, and so refused to provide the reinforcements demanded. The idea of a flexible, aggressive defence based on manoeuvre was condemned. German troops were to stand firm and die in position, or recover lost ground by immediate counter-attacks. These orders tied the hands of the German commanders. As *General der Infanterie* (General of Infantry) Günther Blumentritt, Chief of Staff at OB West commented: 'There was no plan any longer.' The policy was one of rigid defence at all costs.

With the fall of Cherbourg in late June, St-Lô became much more important to both sides. Army Group B correctly predicted that the main American effort would now be to seize the line St-Lô–Coutances as a base for a break-out to the south. When this thrust was blocked in early July, the Germans believed that further attacks would be launched along the Vire. In the face of these threats, their aim was to hold St-Lô as long as possible, for moral

German Formations in the Battle for St-Lô
(principal units only)

Seventh Army *Generaloberst Friedrich Dollmann* (died 28 June)
SS-Oberstgruppenführer Paul Hausser (28 June–)

II Paratroop Corps *Gen der Fallschirmtruppen Eugen Meindl*
12th Paratroop Reconnaissance Btn — *Hauptmann Bodo Göttsche*
12th Paratroop Assault Gun Brigade — *Hauptmann Günther Gersteuer*

3rd Paratroop Division *GenLt Richard Schimpf*
5th Paratroop Regiment — *Major Karl Heinz Becker*
8th Paratroop Regiment — *Oberst Ernst Liebach*
9th Paratroop Regiment — *Major Kurt Stephani*
I/3rd Paratroop Artillery Regiment — *Hauptmann Fleischmann*
3rd Paratroop Anti-Tank Battalion — *Hauptmann Persch*
3rd Paratroop Engineer Battalion — *Major Karl Beth*

352nd Infantry Division *GenLt Dietrich Kraiss*
914th Grenadier Regiment — *OberstLt Ernst Heyna*
915th Grenadier Regiment — *OberstLt Karl Meyer*
916th Grenadier Regiment — *Oberst Ernst Goth*
352nd Artillery Regiment — *OberstLt Karl-Wilhelm Ocker*
352nd Anti-Tank Battalion — *Hauptmann Jahn*
352nd Engineer Battalion
352nd Fusilier Battalion

Units attached to II Paratroop Corps (principally to 352nd Inf Div)

30th Mobile Brigade *OberstLt von Aufsess*

1st Anti-Aircraft Assault Regt (elements) *Oberst Paul von Kistowski*

726th Grenadier Regiment *Oberst Walter Korfes*

Battlegroup *Böhm* (from 353rd Infantry Division)
II/943rd Grenadier Regiment; 353rd Fusilier Battalion.

Battlegroup *Kentner* (from 266th Infantry Division)
Staff 897th Grenadier Regiment; I and II/897th Grenadier Regiment;
13/897th Grenadier Regiment; 3/, 8/ and 9/266th Artillery Regiment;
one platoon infantry anti-tank guns.
*(Some sources claim further reinforcements from this division, notably
II and III/899th Grenadier Regiment.)*

Battlegroup *Rambach* (from 343rd Infantry Division)
III/898th Infantry Regiment; I/343rd Engineer Battalion;
7/343rd Artillery Regiment; one platoon infantry anti-tank guns.

LXXXIV Corps *Gen der Artillerie Erich Marcks* (died 12 June)
Gen der Artillerie Wilhelm Fahrmbacher (to 18 June)
GenLt Dietrich von Choltitz (from 18 June)

Panzer Lehr Division *GenLt Fritz Bayerlein*
(See table on p. 79)

5th Paratroop Division

	GenLt Gustav Wilke
13th Paratroop Regiment	*OberstLt Wolf Werner,*
	Graf von der Schulenburg
14th Paratroop Regiment	*Major Herbert Noster*
15th Paratroop Regiment	*Oberst Kurt Gröschke*
I/5th Paratroop Artillery Regiment	*Oberst Winzer*
5th Paratroop Anti-Tank Battalion	*Hauptmann Rolf Müller*
5th Paratroop Engineer Battalion	*Hauptmann Gerhard Mertins*
5th Paratroop Anti-Aircraft Battalion	*Hauptmann Fritz Görtz*

17th SS Panzergrenadier Division *Götz von Berlichingen*

Elements, principally 38th SS Panzergrenadier Regiment

Battlegroup *Heintz* (from 275th Infantry Division)

I and II/984th Grenadier Regiment; 275th Engineer Battalion;
275th Fusilier Battalion; III/275th Artillery Regt; 275th Anti-Tank Coy;
one platoon infantry howitzers; one platoon infantry anti-tank guns

Engineer Battalion 'Angers'

Notes: Apart from 5th Paratroop Division, part of which fought in the western
part of LXXXIV Corps' sector, only units that fought east of the River Taute
are identified. Formations shifted between corps according to circumstances;
for example, 352nd Infantry Division began as part of LXXXIV Corps, but
spent most of the battle with II Paratroop Corps, which is why it is listed
under this heading. 5th Paratroop Division fought as sub-units, some of them
in II Paratroop Corps' area; it is listed under LXXXIV Corps because this is
the headquarters to which most of the division was subordinated. Several
units destroyed before 8 June or which only spent a short time in the battle
area (e.g. from 2nd SS Panzer Division) are not listed. Some corps-level units
(mainly artillery) are also not identified.

Fallschirmjäger. These German paratroop infantry were amongst the most
resolute of St-Lô's defenders. *(Bundesarchiv [BA] 1011-576-1846-19A)*

and psychological reasons as well as strategic calculations. Attempts to create a mobile reserve in Seventh Army for a major counter-attack, however, failed, and the inexorable US advance resumed.

During mid-July, the defences of St-Lô were compromised east and west of the Vire by US successes, and a *coup de main* pre-empted a last attempt at close defence on 18 July. Attempts to counter-attack the town from the south were feeble and unenthusiastic. Seventh Army fell back to reorganise and await Bradley's next offensive. When it came a week later, the effects were devastating.

THE BALANCE OF FORCES

The Americans had various advantages during the battle for St-Lô. One of the greatest lay in First Army's tactical air support. Unlike the heavily-outnumbered *Luftwaffe*, which rarely made sorties to western Normandy, on each fine day US troops could have close air support. Allied air power dominated the German rear areas, delaying and reducing reinforcements and supply columns coming

The temporary grave of *General der Artillerie* Erich Marcks, killed by an American fighter-bomber on 12 June. *(USNA)*

up. Aircraft also attacked the German command structure; on 12 June *General der Artillerie* (General of Artillery) Erich Marcks, commander of LXXXIV Corps, was killed in a fighter-bomber attack, while Rommel himself was seriously wounded by a Spitfire on 17 July.

First Army also had the advantages of numbers, material, standardisation of organisation and equipment. Whereas US forces built up rapidly and received replacements for their battle casualties, Seventh Army was deprived of adequate reinforcement and replacements by strategic policy and the effects of Allied air power. Those

personnel who did arrive were often in small groups rather than fully organised formations. The Germans were also constantly short of matériel, particularly ammunition. They had numerous different types of weapons, including much French- and Russian-made artillery, and according to one source had to find 252 types of ammunition. Much of their transport was horse-drawn, motor vehicles were of many types, and some were requisitioned civilian models. Consequently supply was complicated.

US equipment was modern and standardised, which made supply relatively simple; the Americans managed the business side of war much better. Some German weapons were superior to the American, some inferior. German tanks, particularly the Panzer V Panther, were better than the Sherman, but were vulnerable in the *bocage* to US tank destroyers and the infantry's bazookas. The principal German machine gun, the MG 42, had a much higher rate of fire than the American Browning Automatic Rifle (BAR), but US troops carried a better rifle (the M-1 Garand) and grenades. The mortars of both sides were similar. First Army's artillery was greatly superior to the German, particularly in its fire control techniques and close co-operation with infantry. The use of air observation enhanced its accuracy and effectiveness in a – literally – striking way.

USAAF P-47 Thunderbolt fighter-bombers prepare to take off. Allied air superiority was a critical factor in the Battle of Normandy, although poor weather and the difficulty of identifying targets in the *bocage* reduced its influence somewhat during the struggle for St-Lô. *(USNA)*

The quality of the soldiers and units on the German side was extremely variable. The best formations sent to St-Lô, such as Panzer Lehr Division, were very highly skilled; others were less able. Some, such as 3rd Paratroop Division, were highly trained and fanatically motivated. 352nd Infantry Division was a solid formation, with experienced officers and NCOs, but the men of some units were medically unfit for field service and others were unreliable. The 'German' forces in Normandy also included many men who were not native Germans, notably several '*Ost*' ('East') battalions of former Soviet prisoners of war. Many Poles, pressed into the German Army, were also keen to defect.

Quality was more consistent on the American side. Training of soldiers was standardised, as was unit and formation organisation. Some formations had combat experience, and benefited from it, but the others caught up. Initially the German troops had the great advantage of familiarity with the ground, but American soldiers learned to adapt their tactics and develop equipment in ingenious ways to solve the problems of fighting in the *bocage*.

CHAPTER 2

OPERATIONS EAST OF THE VIRE, 8–20 JUNE

After the near-disaster of D-Day (See 'Battle Zone Normandy' *Omaha Beach*), by nightfall on 7 June Maj Gen Gerow's V Corps had broken the back of German resistance in its invasion sector. On its right flank 29th Infantry Division was moving west to join with VII Corps from Utah Beach, and to reach its D-Day objectives along the north bank of the Aure. Meanwhile, to the east Maj Gen Clarence R. Huebner's 1st Infantry Division was approaching a junction with Second (British) Army along the Drôme. Particularly rapid progress was made by 18th Infantry Regiment, whose 2nd and 3rd Battalions (2/18th and 3/18th) crossed the Aure east of Trévières during the afternoon. Opposition from the German 352nd Infantry Division was negligible. Nevertheless, the Germans hung on at Trévières (HQ of 916th Grenadier Regiment), hoping to make the town a bastion around which they could rebuild their defences.

During 8 June US troops accelerated their advance, bolstered by the arrival of Maj Gen Walter Robertson's 2nd Infantry Division, disembarking on Omaha Beach. An attempt by 1st Infantry Division to envelop a German battlegroup was only partly successful, with many of the Germans escaping south across the N13. However, at last light a link-up was achieved with British commandos near Port-en-Bessin. Despite weakening resistance, concern about the imminent arrival of German reserves made Gerow anxious to secure his flanks. V Corps also wanted to pre-empt the creation of a new front near Trévières, from which German artillery could hit Omaha Beach. Consequently, at 1700 hours US commanders were told that further offensive operations would be required the following day.

After the bloody battle for Omaha Beach, resistance to V Corps' advance was generally sporadic and of limited effectiveness. Here a German prisoner is searched on 10 June. *(USNA)*

A few hours later V Corps Field Order No. 2 was issued, ordering a major attack on 9 June. This would involve all three of Gerow's divisions, with 29th Infantry Division driving west to contact VII Corps, and south across the River Aure towards St-Lô. Further east 2nd Infantry Division was to capture Trévières, cross the River Tortonne and advance to the Cerisy Forest, 13 km to the south,

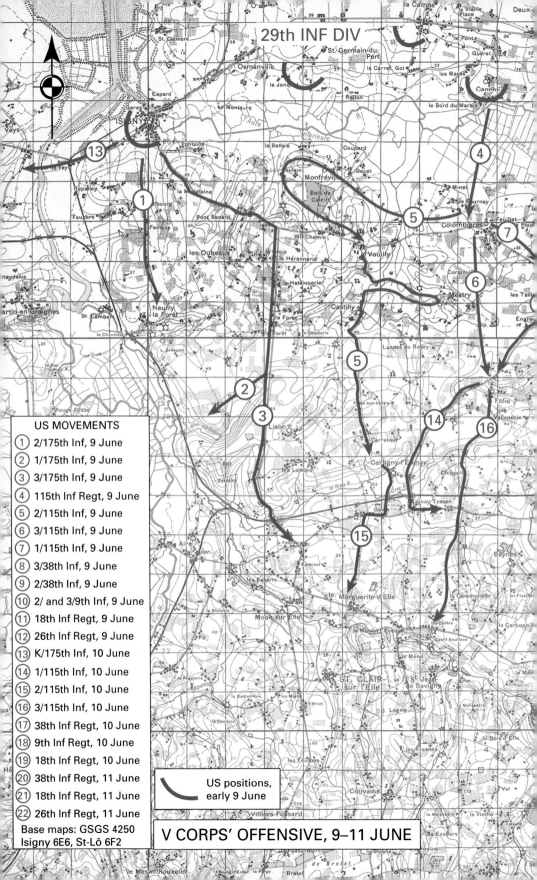

29th INF DIV

US MOVEMENTS
1. 2/175th Inf, 9 June
2. 1/175th Inf, 9 June
3. 3/175th Inf, 9 June
4. 115th Inf Regt, 9 June
5. 2/115th Inf, 9 June
6. 3/115th Inf, 9 June
7. 1/115th Inf, 9 June
8. 3/38th Inf, 9 June
9. 2/38th Inf, 9 June
10. 2/ and 3/9th Inf, 9 June
11. 18th Inf Regt, 9 June
12. 26th Inf Regt, 9 June
13. K/175th Inf, 10 June
14. 1/115th Inf, 10 June
15. 2/115th Inf, 10 June
16. 3/115th Inf, 10 June
17. 38th Inf Regt, 10 June
18. 9th Inf Regt, 10 June
19. 18th Inf Regt, 10 June
20. 38th Inf Regt, 11 June
21. 18th Inf Regt, 11 June
22. 26th Inf Regt, 11 June

Base maps: GSGS 4250
Isigny 6E6, St-Lô 6F2

US positions,
early 9 June

V CORPS' OFFENSIVE, 9–11 JUNE

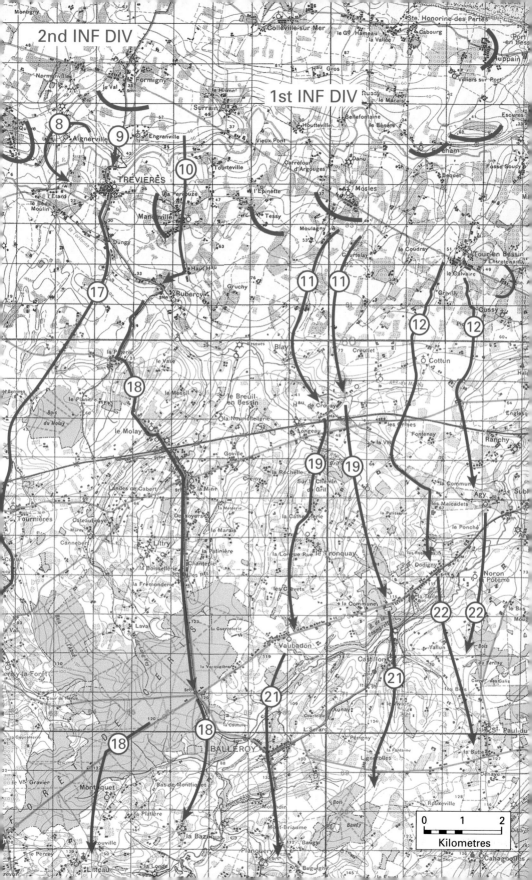

which was considered a likely assembly area for German counter-attacks. On 2nd Division's left, 1st Infantry Division was to cut the road between Bayeux and le Molay-Littry (now the D5) and seize high ground along the River Drôme. The division would also secure the highway from Bayeux to St-Lô (the D572), thus blocking any attempt to attack Second (British) Army from the south-west.

To halt the anticipated offensive, on 8 June Seventh Army directed 352nd Division to stand firm while forces assembled for a counter-attack from St-Lô. This was to be carried out by *General der Fallschirmtruppen* (General of Paratroops) Eugen Meindl's II Paratroop Corps, *en route* from Brittany and comprising 3rd Paratroop Division, 17th SS Panzergrenadier Division *Götz von Berlichingen* and 77th Infantry Division. Almost immediately, however, 77th Infantry Division was detached to prevent a collapse on the Cotentin peninsula, weakening the intended drive. As Seventh Army's war diary observed:

> 'Accomplishment of this [counter-attack], however, is questionable, since the arrival of the approaching elements is uncertain in terms of timing and degree of coordination and the newly arrived elements must be thrown into the battle as they arrive.'
>
> *Source:* Seventh Army War Diary, 9 June, RG 407, Box 24154, Folder 488, US National Archives (USNA).

THE 1ST AND 2ND DIVISION FRONT

Operations in the eastern zone of V Corps' area began around midday on 9 June, when 1st Infantry Division attacked from its positions along the N13. Little opposition was met, and 3/26th Infantry thrust 7 km to Agy (on the D572) by nightfall. Further west 2/26th and its accompanying tanks reached Dodigny (Noron-la-Poterie on modern maps) soon after midnight. Colonel G. Smith's 18th Infantry Regiment also made good progress, pushing to the eastern edge of the Cerisy Forest by dawn on the 10th. According to one German account, the commander of the 726th Grenadier Regiment, *Oberst* (Colonel) Walter Korfes, was captured during these attacks. However, claims that Allied air operations assisted the advance can be discounted, as the weather on 9 June was poor and prevented most Allied aircraft from taking to the skies.

In 2nd Infantry Division's sector the attack initially was less successful. With much of its heavy equipment still coming ashore,

9th Infantry Regiment laboured for most of the day to bypass 916th Grenadiers' defences near Trévières and attain its first objectives along the Tortonne. Assaults by 38th Infantry also met intense resistance at Trévières itself. Despite powerful artillery support little progress was made. However, following an outflanking move by 29th Infantry Division to the west (*see pp. 36–7*), the Germans abandoned their positions, and the following morning Trévières fell without a struggle. Maj Gen Robertson's troops then began a lightning advance, driving south to le Molay-Littry and Cerisy-le-Forêt almost unopposed. By the end of 10 June 9th Infantry was through the Cerisy Forest near Balleroy, with 38th Infantry on the western edge of the forest only 2 km from the River Elle. German reconnaissance parties offered scant opposition, and withdrew before the American blow.

A patrol moves cautiously into an orchard to clear a German position. *(USNA)*

By now 352nd Infantry Division had been reinforced by elements of *Oberstleutnant* (Lieutenant Colonel – Lt Col) Freiherr von Aufsess' 30th Mobile Brigade, comprising about 900 cyclists. The brigade deployed on a 6-km front along the north–south stretch of the Elle west of Cerisy-la-Forêt. The leading detachments of 3rd Paratroop Division had also arrived. Their scouts had infiltrated into the Cerisy Forest on 10 June and decided that the Americans were not yet there in strength. The divisional commander, GenLt

Richard Schimpf, was confident he could occupy the north edge of the woods, as ordered. But, owing to the collapse of 352nd Infantry Division, his orders were changed. Instead of counter-attacking, the paratroopers deployed in a string of positions from St-Germain-d'Elle, 4 km south of the western tip of the Cerisy Forest, via Bérigny and Couvains to the north-west. Nevertheless, the situation appeared critical, since Schimpf's men had little artillery and only tenuous contact with 352nd Infantry Division on the left and 17th SS Panzergrenadier Division's reconnaissance battalion on the right.

Looking back on this period Schimpf remarked: 'If the Americans, at that time, had launched an energetic attack from the Forest of Cerisy, St-Lô would have fallen.' But V Corps' advance was slowing. 2nd Infantry Division had gained 17 km on 10 June and now the soldiers were tired and supply lines were stretched. The Americans were also unsure of the location of 17th SS Panzergrenadier Division, and concerned that the presence of its reconnaissance battalion near Balleroy indicated preparations for an attack. In fact, on 10 June Seventh Army decided to send 17th SS Division to bolster the front near Carentan. This left a 16-km gap between 3rd Paratroop Division at Bérigny and Panzer Lehr Division (from I SS Panzer Corps) near Tilly-sur-Seulles. Although the Germans intended bringing up 2nd Panzer Division to fill this gap, and reinforcing the St-Lô sector with 353rd Infantry Division from Brittany, this would not happen for several days. But V Corps did not know this, and spent 11 June consolidating and patrolling, instead of continuing south. The Germans were grateful and used the day to bring up more troops and strengthen their defences.

By the evening of 11 June Maj Gen Gerow was ready to resume the offensive, and issued Field Order No. 3. This directed renewed attacks on the 12th, with 29th Infantry Division crossing the Elle in the west and then driving towards St-Lô. Further east, 2nd Infantry Division's 23rd Infantry was also to cross the Elle, seizing Hill 192 some 4 km west of Bérigny. This high ground controlled the surrounding countryside and was seen as the key to the eastern approaches to St-Lô. Other divisional elements would push south towards St-Germain-d'Elle. The deepest penetration, however, would occur on the left, where 1st Infantry Division was to capture Caumont-l'Éventé, 10 km south of Balleroy. Caumont was an important communications centre, located on another piece of dominating terrain. Possession of the town was seen as a particularly important objective for V Corps' attack.

An aerial view of Caumont, showing the *bocage* country to the south. American vehicles can be seen in the town. *(Imperial War Museum CL 611)*

At 0800 hours on 12 June the Americans advanced, supported by artillery and tanks. Little resistance was met on 1st Division's front, and by the morning of the 13th it had captured Caumont and cut the road to St-Lô to the west. However, 2nd Infantry Division faced much greater opposition from troops of 3rd Paratroop Division and 30th Mobile Brigade. Although 9th Infantry Regiment reached the Elle without too much difficulty, 23rd Infantry struggled to make progress north of Bérigny. Artillery and air bombardment failed to open a route forward, and 1/23rd was able to establish only a small bridgehead over the Elle east of St-Jean-de-Savigny. Despite reinforcement the next day by 38th Infantry and thousands of rounds of artillery support, by the end of 13 June US forces had still not captured St-Georges-D'Elle. Having lost 540 men since the start of the operation, 2nd Division was ordered to halt its attack and reorganize for defence.

Late on 13 June Lt Gen Bradley ordered a suspension of the US drive towards St-Lô. He thought that further attacks might deprive First Army of resources needed for the capture of Cherbourg, which was his main objective. Reports that reconnaissance troops from 2nd Panzer Division had been engaged near Caumont on 13 June also indicated a possible German counter-attack. Since British XXX Corps was involved in a pitched battle the same day at Villers-Bocage, 11 km east of Caumont, Bradley was reluctant to order his forces to extend their salient to the south. Furthermore, the arrival of US XIX Corps on V Corps' right flank necessitated a re-arrangement of First Army's command responsibilities. V Corps was therefore ordered to hold its positions and dig in. However, Gerow's Field Order No. 5, issued on 13 June, also stated that local attacks could be mounted to improve defensive positions and to divert German attention from operations on the Cotentin peninsula. With this in mind, 2nd Infantry Division began planning further offensive operations in the direction of St-Lô.

On 16 June 2nd Infantry Division attacked again. In the morning 2/9th Infantry moved against St-Germain-d'Elle, but was stopped by a strongpoint among the hedgerows. 23rd Infantry Regiment advanced into Bérigny, but suffered 173 casualties and was held on the Elle to the west. The greatest effort, however, was made by 38th Infantry, supported by the divisional engineer battalion, which assaulted St-Georges-d'Elle and Hill 192. L Company managed to get halfway up the northern slope, but 2/38th was halted on the right by the hard-fighting German paratroopers. Although 3/38th's commander, Lt Col Olinto Barsanti, insisted his men could hold the hill, Maj Gen Robertson ordered a withdrawal. As an American historian noted, only with 'careful and meticulous planning' was the enemy likely to be dislodged from this critical piece of terrain.

V Corps had reached the culminating point of its attack, and came to rest on 17 June. 2nd Infantry Division held a front line of 9 km from north of St-Georges-d'Elle via Bérigny and St-Germain-d'Elle to the Drôme near Cormolain. 1st Infantry Division held Caumont, and was in contact with Second (British) Army on its left. Further north, 2nd Armored Division was in reserve in the Cerisy Forest. V Corps conducted aggressive patrols and harassed the Germans with artillery, but made no major attacks. Meanwhile, the staffs went on to devise a training scheme for all-arms tactics and also studied the problem of capturing Hill 192.

For their part the Germans could draw some satisfaction from their recent combat performance. 3rd Paratroop Division had proved itself a first-rate unit, and its three paratroop regiments (5th, 8th and 9th) faced 2nd Infantry Division confident in their ability to repulse further attacks. The unit commanders were aggressive and active, using patrols, infiltration and raids for field training. They were also eager to cure their soldiers of 'tank terror', training them to use the *Panzerfaust* anti-tank weapon at minimum range. The soldiers also dug deep to improve their defences.

A US Signals Corps soldier operates a field telephone, 9 June. His .30-calibre carbine lies close to hand. *(USNA)*

THE 29TH DIVISION FRONT

On 8 June, 352nd Infantry Division was falling back from a front extending from Grandcamp-Maisy to Bayeux. The divisional commander, GenLt Dietrich Kraiss, ordered his scattered units to withdraw south of the Aure, conducting a flexible defence to gain time. He believed that the flooded valley of the Aure would be a serious obstacle to US V Corps. His troops were therefore deployed to cover possible crossing points, particularly at Isigny, Monfréville, Colombières and Bricqueville. Company and platoon groups were also left north of the Aure at la Cambe, Authenay and Cardonville, to delay the Americans as they sought to expand their beachhead.

By now, however, Maj Gen Charles H. Gerhardt's 29th Infantry Division had the bit between its teeth. On 8 June 115th Infantry Regiment, ordered to move south to the Aure, occupied Longueville and sent out reconnaissance parties. Simultaneously Colonel Paul Goode's 175th Infantry Regiment moved west along the north bank, clearing pockets of resistance as it went. The 175th was driven on by Maj Gen Gerhardt and his assistant, Brigadier General (Brig Gen) Norman D. Cota. Gerhardt was convinced the Germans had abandoned Isigny and was determined to seize it. Very early on 9 June, after a night march, elements of 175th Infantry and 747th Tank Battalion entered Isigny and rushed the bridge across the Aure. Only a few snipers opposed them. Men from 439th *Ost* Battalion ran away without blowing up the bridge, gunners from two German batteries leaving their guns behind and following them.

A US military policeman inspects a German headquarters at St-Clair-sur-l'Elle. The scattered papers, duty roster and open bottles all suggest a hurried departure by the previous occupants. Neither do they appear to have been keen to take with them the inspirational print of Hitler. *(USNA)*

Following Maj Gen Gerow's orders, 29th Infantry Division prepared to cross the River Aure. As described in detail in Tour A *(pp. 122–35)*, during the night of 8/9 June a reconnaissance party found German sentries on the south bank of the river opposite Canchy asleep, and reported back by sunrise. On the morning of 9 June 1/115th advanced onto the causeway south of Écrammeville, but was halted by machine-gun fire from Trévières. 3/115th, followed by 2/115th and then 1/115th, crossed the Aure further west, assisted by 121st Engineer Combat Battalion, which built footbridges over the most difficult water obstacles. The Americans then fanned out before driving south towards the River Elle. By nightfall 3/115th Infantry was at la Folie, 5 km beyond the Aure, with 1/115th in Bricqueville. Meanwhile 2/115th moved south towards le Carrefour des Vignes aux Gendres. Rapid progress was also made by 175th Infantry Regiment, advancing from Isigny along the D11 towards St-Lô. Despite determined resistance at la Forêt, where the Germans fought to protect the evacuation of an important supply dump, by midnight the 175th's leading elements were at la Fotelaie, a few kilometres east of the Vire and barely a thousand metres north of the bridge at Moon-sur-Elle.

The troops of the German 352nd Infantry Division were shocked and anxious. All their units were under pressure, and the division had no reserve. GenLt Kraiss expected 1/115th Infantry to link up with 2nd Infantry Division at Bernesq (on the River Esque), encircling the battlegroup at Trévières. When LXXXIV Corps heard that the line of the Aure had been lost, 352nd Division was ordered to retire 11 km to defend the Elle. However, Kraiss reported that his division could not hold this river – which was only a few metres wide – since it had insufficient infantry and artillery and no explosives to blow the bridges. In response the division was given two battle-groups of anti-aircraft gunners and told to hold the road crossings.

During the night of 9–10 June 352nd Infantry Division withdrew south. GenLt Kraiss's headquarters left Littry at 0300 hours and reached le Mesnil-Rouxelin two hours later. By 0630 hours German staff officers were moving out to contact the battlegroups. Parts of 914th Grenadiers, with about 500 men (mostly artillerymen without guns), held 4 km along the Elle with their left flank on the River Vire. Further east, 916th Grenadier Regiment occupied 7 km with 1,000 men. During 10 June some detachments appeared to help fill the gaps, and in the evening they got more reinforcements. Meanwhile, 3rd Paratroop Division began to deploy on their right.

Gerhardt's division suffered an unfortunate encounter during the night of 9–10 June. Both 2/115th and 3/115th Infantry had used their opportunity to move south unopposed. But when 3/115th reached its objective, 2/115th carried on. Shortly after midnight the battalion began turning into fields just south of le Carrefour des Vignes aux Gendres to rest. Troops still on the road at the rear

US Formations in the Battle for St-Lô
(principal organic units only)

First US Army — *Lt Gen Omar N. Bradley*

V Corps — *Maj Gen Leonard T. Gerow*

1st Infantry Division 'Big Red One' — *Maj Gen Clarence R. Huebner*
- 16th Infantry Regiment — *Colonel George A. Taylor*
- 18th Infantry Regiment — *Colonel George Smith, Jr.*
- 26th Infantry Regiment — *Colonel John F.R. Seitz*

1st Reconnaissance Troop; 1st Engineer Combat Battalion
5th Artillery Battalion (155-mm howitzer)
7th, 32nd, 33rd Field Artillery Battalions (105-mm howitzer)

2nd Infantry Division 'Indian Head' — *Maj Gen Walter M. Robertson*
- 9th Infantry Regiment — *Colonel Chester J. Hirschfelder*
- 23rd Infantry Regiment — *Colonel Hurley E. Fuller*
- 38th Infantry Regiment — *Colonel Walter A. Elliott*

2nd Reconnaissance Troop; 2nd Engineer Combat Battalion
12th Field Artillery Battalion (155-mm howitzer)
15th, 37th, 38th Field Artillery Battalions (105-mm howitzer)

VII Corps — *Maj Gen J. Lawton Collins*

9th Infantry Division 'Hitler's Nemesis' — *Maj Gen Manton S. Eddy*
- 39th Infantry Regiment — *Colonel Harry A. Flint*
- 47th Infantry Regiment — *Colonel George W. Smythe*
- 60th Infantry Regiment — *Colonel Jesse L. Gibney*

9th Reconnaissance Troop; 15th Engineer Combat Battalion
34th Artillery Battalion (155-mm howitzer)
26th, 60th, 84th Field Artillery Battalions (105-mm howitzer)

XIX Corps — *Maj Gen Charles Corlett*

29th Infantry Division 'Blue and Gray' — *Maj Gen Charles H. Gerhardt*
- 115th Infantry Regiment — *Colonel Eugene N. Slappey*
- 116th Infantry Regiment — *Colonel Charles D. W. Canham*
- 175th Infantry Regiment — *Colonel Paul R. Goode*

29th Reconnaissance Troop; 121st Engineer Combat Battalion
227th Field Artillery Battalion (155-mm howitzer)
110th, 111th, 224th Field Artillery Battalions (105-mm howitzer)

of the column heard vehicles and believed other US troops were coming to link up, but a group of Germans had been retreating behind 2/115th, and at about 0200 hours they attacked. The bivouac area was illuminated by flares, then hit by fire from assault guns, mortars and small arms. The battalion lost 150 men killed, wounded or missing. Hundreds of others scattered into the hedgerows. In the morning, however, 2/115th regrouped, received replacements, and resumed its march south. The rest of the regiment

30th Infantry Division 'Old Hickory'   *Maj Gen Leland S. Hobbs*

  117th Infantry Regiment   *Colonel Henry Kelly*
  119th Infantry Regiment   *Colonel Alfred V. Ednie*
  120th Infantry Regiment   *Colonel Hammond Birks*

  30th Reconnaissance Troop
  105th Engineer Combat Battalion
  113th Field Artillery Battalion (155-mm howitzer)
  118th, 197th, 230th Field Artillery Battalions (105-mm howitzer)

35th Infantry Division 'Santa Fe'   *Maj Gen Paul W. Baade*

  134th Infantry Regiment   *Colonel Butler B. Miltonburger*
  137th Infantry Regiment   *Colonel Grant Layng*
  320th Infantry Regiment   *Colonel Bernard A. Byrne*

  35th Reconnaissance Troop
  60th Engineer Combat Battalion
  127th Field Artillery Battalion (155-mm howitzer)
  161st, 216th, 219th Field Artillery Battalions (105-mm howitzer)

3rd Armored Division 'Spearhead'   *Maj Gen Leroy H. Watson*

  HQ Combat Command A   *Brig Gen Doyle O. Hickey*
  HQ Combat Command B   *Brig Gen John H. Bohn*
  32nd, 33rd Armored Regiments
  36th Armored Infantry Regiment

  83rd Armored Reconnaissance Battalion
  23rd Armored Engineer Battalion
  54th, 67th, 391st Armored Field Artillery Battalions

Notes: Only units that fought east of the River Taute are identified. US formations shifted between corps according to circumstances; for example, 29th Infantry Division began as part of V Corps, but spent most of the battle with XIX Corps, which it why it is listed under this heading. US divisions often had numerous attached units and sub-units. Some of these (especially tank battalions attached to infantry divisions) remained with the division throughout the struggle for St-Lô; others spent only a few days attached. Given their number, and considerations of space, none are listed here. Some of the more important attached units, however, are identified where appropriate in the narrative and battlefield tours. Several units which played only a fleeting or indirect role in the battle (e.g. 2nd Armored Division, 101st Airborne Division) are not listed. Commanding Officers are those in charge of the unit on the date of its entry into the battle for St-Lô; a good proportion of these were replaced, wounded or – in one case – captured. For reasons of space, replacements are not listed.

also moved forward and by the evening of 10 June was deployed north of the Elle, with elements of 175th Infantry on its right.

On 11 June 352nd Infantry Division received orders from Seventh Army that the Elle must be held 'under all circumstances'. However, in accordance with Gerow's Field Order No. 3, Maj Gen Gerhardt was planning an attack on 12 June by Colonel Eugene Slappey's 115th Infantry Regiment to cross the Elle, secure St-Clair-sur-l'Elle, and go on to Couvains. This would protect the right flank of 2nd

Infantry Division in its advance towards Hill 192. Meanwhile 175th Infantry Regiment would defend its positions to the west. The division's third regiment, 116th Infantry (supported by 747th Tank Battalion), was to move up to Ste-Marguerite-d'Elle, ready to exploit success.

The Germans were also preparing, by digging deep shelters along the hedgerows on the steep south bank. Dispersed machine-gun posts in the first line could deliver fire along the stream and rake the north bank. Observers in concealed bunkers directed fire from mortars and howitzers positioned on reverse slopes to the rear. Behind these, screened from view, were denser field-works in the main line of resistance. Further back, local reserves – including some armoured vehicles – waited to cover a retirement or go forward in counter-attacks.

Looking south across the Elle near Ste-Marguerite. On these slopes 1/115th Infantry was halted and pinned by fire from 352nd Infantry Division on the opposite side. *(Author)*

The American bombardment opened at 0330 hours on 12 June and continued for 90 minutes. When 1/115th and 3/115th Infantry tried to cross the river, however, they found the Germans very active. Major James Morris' 1/115th was pinned by machine-gun and artillery fire, losing 100 men without getting across the creek. A kilometre to the east 3/115th was hit by a concentration of mortar and artillery fire while forming up, and suffered many casualties. Elements of its companies went forward, crossed the Elle and plunged into the *bocage*. About 3 km further south, near les Fresnes, the Americans found themselves isolated, surrounded and low on ammunition. When attempts to provide tank support failed they were ordered to withdraw, but not everyone made it back to the Elle. Altogether, 3/115th lost 66 men killed, 138 wounded and 16 missing during the day. These were grievous losses by any standards.

The bridge at Moulin Jourdan, looking south. On 12 June a platoon of Shermans from 747th Tank Battalion tried to cross the Elle here to reinforce 3/115th Infantry, but lost three tanks to gunfire and mines, and withdrew. *(Simon Trew [ST])*

Enraged by the performance of the 115th, Gerhardt sacked Colonel Slappey and replaced him with the divisional Chief of Staff, Colonel Godwin Ordway. He also ordered 116th Infantry Regiment to assault the river without benefit of briefing or reconnaissance. Colonel Charles Canham's 116th Infantry accordingly attacked at 1930 hours, surprised the Germans and pushed on 2 km south.

On 13 June 116th Regiment, with 3/115th attached, attacked St-Clair-sur-l'Elle and exploited south. Both sides were confused by a thick morning mist, but it protected the Americans from German fire. Supported by a barrage from 29th Division's artillery, 2/116th captured St-Clair and 1/116th took Couvains; 3/115th and 3/116th Infantry then advanced to consolidate. Meanwhile 115th Infantry sent patrols across the Elle, which took prisoners and reported a German withdrawal. Further west 175th Infantry was barely contained by Battlegroup *Heyna* (elements of 914th Grenadiers under *Oberstleutnant* Ernst Heyna). Gerhardt felt that

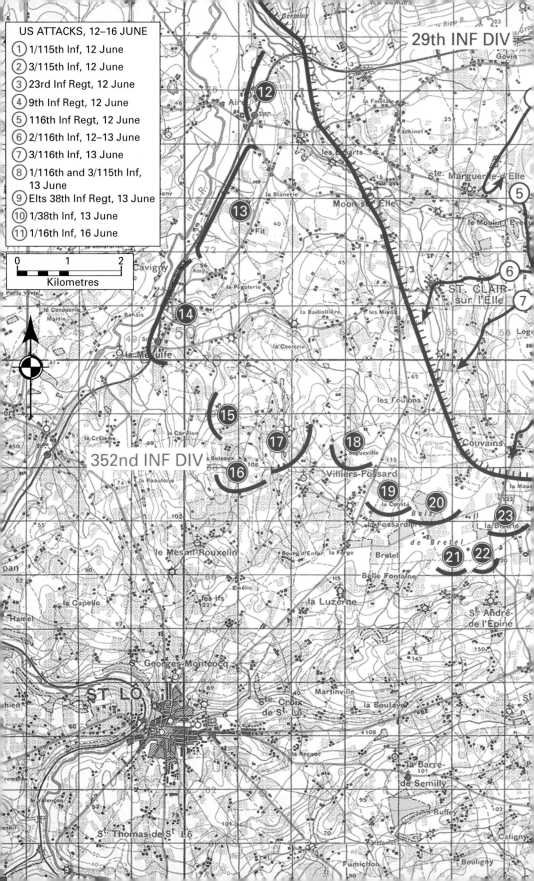

US ATTACKS, 12–16 JUNE

① 1/115th Inf, 12 June
② 3/115th Inf, 12 June
③ 23rd Inf Regt, 12 June
④ 9th Inf Regt, 12 June
⑤ 116th Inf Regt, 12 June
⑥ 2/116th Inf, 12–13 June
⑦ 3/116th Inf, 13 June
⑧ 1/116th and 3/115th Inf, 13 June
⑨ Elts 38th Inf Regt, 13 June
⑩ 1/38th Inf, 13 June
⑪ 1/16th Inf, 16 June

0   1   2
Kilometres

29th INF DIV

352nd INF DIV

EAST OF THE VIRE, 12–18 JUNE

Front line, end 14 June
Front line, end 18 June
Base map: GSGS 4250 St-Lô 6F2

US POSITIONS, END 18 JUNE

12 L/117th Inf
13 3/119th Inf
14 1/119th Inf
15 2/175th Inf
16 3/175th Inf
17 1/175th Inf
18 3/115th Inf
19 2/115th Inf
20 1/115th Inf
21 3/116th Inf
22 1/116th Inf
23 2/116th Inf
24 2/38th Inf
25 3/38th Inf
26 1/23rd Inf
27 Elts 23rd Inf Regt
28 Elts 9th Inf Regt
29 2/9th Inf
30 2/16th Inf
31 3/18th Inf

2nd INF DIV

1st INF DIV

3rd PARA DIV

352nd Infantry Division was about to break, and that he could take St-Lô within a couple of days if allowed to push on.

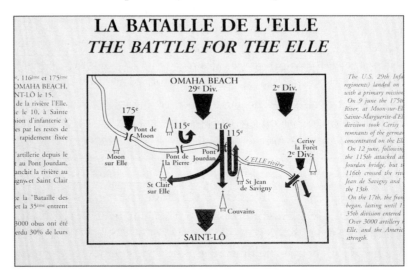

Map of the Elle battle, 12–13 June. This map is part of the 29th Division memorial beside the D54 at le Mesnil, 600 metres south of the river crossing at Moulin Jourdan. *(ST)*

The Germans agreed. On 14 June, at a Seventh Army conference, LXXXIV Corps reported that 352nd Infantry Division was 'at the end of its resources and should be relieved.' Battlegroup *Heyna* was under strain, Battlegroup *Goth* (916th Grenadiers) was falling back from St-Clair-sur-l'Elle, and Battlegroup *von Aufsess* (30th Mobile Brigade) had lost Couvains. 3rd Paratroop Division and 353rd Infantry Division (which was arriving to join the battle) were not yet fully deployed. St-Lô could be lost next day.

However, Gerhardt was restrained by Bradley, concerned that 29th Infantry Division might outrun its strength and supplies. The division had suffered 2,400 casualties (mostly among its infantry) since 6 June. Maj Gen Charles Corlett, commander of the new XIX Corps to which 29th Infantry Division was transferred on 14 June, ordered Gerhardt to hold back until the newly arrived 30th Infantry Division could be deployed to the west. 29th Infantry Division halted, dug in and sent out patrols. The exhausted German battlegroups restored their intermittent lines of defence.

The expected US offensive developed on Friday 16 June all along the front. To the east 2nd Infantry Division attacked Hill 192, while to the west 30th Infantry Division continued its advance towards the Vire–Taute Canal (*see pp. 56–9*). Between them 29th Division attacked on several axes to pin German reserves, and to seize critical terrain north-east of St-Lô. Near the Vire 175th Infantry Regiment began its attack at 0800 hours, pushing Battlegroup *Heyna* back to Amy (l'Hôtel Ballot on modern maps) before noon. 1/175th made the deepest penetration, cutting the road from la Meauffe to St-Clair-sur-l'Elle. Further east, however, the US offensive ran into problems. Although 1/116th Infantry thrust 2 km south from Couvains towards St-André-de-l'Épine, Colonel Canham's other battalions found the going more difficult. Both 2/116th and 3/116th encountered stubborn resistance as they swung west to cut the D6 near Villiers-Fossard. So did the attached 3/115th Infantry, which was thrown back from the hamlet of les Foulons, west of Couvains, during the afternoon. Meanwhile, 115th Regiment's move forward from reserve was complicated by other enemy actions. Some German troops had managed to infiltrate into St-Clair-sur-l'Elle while 2/115th was assembling, and caused considerable disruption. Not until the evening, after a company from 803rd Tank Destroyer Battalion had moved up in support, were the Americans able to secure the town. By then, Maj Gen Corlett had decided to halt 29th Division's advance and consolidate for the night.

The hamlet of les Foulons seen from the north. On 16 June 3/115th Infantry reached these buildings, but was driven back by German counter-attacks to a position west of Couvains. *(Author)*

From the German perspective, however, XIX Corps' attacks had barely been contained. By their own estimate, 45 square kilometres of territory had been lost. Although German troops held the line of the Vire at St-Fromond, they could only damage the bridge there, not demolish it. Meanwhile, Battlegroups *Heyna* and *Goth* had been forced to fall back to the ring of defences east and north of St-Lô.

Fortunately for GenLt Kraiss, however, help was at hand. First, 3rd Paratroop Division, still relatively fresh and strong, extended its front to the west, allowing 352nd Division to form a counter-attack reserve. During the evening of 16 June Seventh Army also committed Battlegroup *Böhm*, comprising 353rd Fusilier Battalion and part of 943rd Grenadier Regiment, from the vanguard of 353rd Infantry Division, to positions around Villiers-Fossard and la Luzerne. A battalion of 122-mm guns also arrived, with sufficient ammunition to lend significant fire support to the defenders.

Gerhardt's troops attacked all along the front again on 17 June, but the Germans resisted more strongly (and may even have received some air support). Although 116th Regiment advanced a short way, its troops became convinced that the Germans had infiltrated between their companies and were about to cut them off, so they halted and dug in. In the afternoon 1/115th advanced along the ridge west from the Bois de Bretel, but was unable to break through at les Forges, on the D6 near Villiers-Fossard. Three kilometres further west 175th Infantry attacked Hill 108 (located on US maps north-west of Villiers-Fossard, but actually with its highest point 1 km south-west of the village), urged on by its new commander, Lt Col Alexander George. Although George himself was wounded, 1/175th's B Company advanced to within a few hundred metres of its objective. However, by this point the battalion was exposed on both flanks: to the west to Germans across the Vire and to the east to Battlegroup *Böhm*, strongly emplaced at Villiers-Fossard.

Bitterly intense close-quarter fighting continued on 18 June. At 0600 hours 175th and 115th Regiments tried to move forward. Despite a heavy preliminary bombardment, 1/ and 3/115th Infantry were stopped within a few fields by German artillery, mortar and machine-gun fire. Lt Col Roger Whiteford's 1/175th did get forward, only to be hit by numerous shells and mortar rounds before being enveloped by a superior force. 1/175th was rapidly isolated, with telephone wires cut and its radio connection with 224th Field Artillery Battalion broken. The infantry from Battlegroup *Böhm* pressed in to within grenade-throwing range. At 1700 hours German armour was heard assembling nearby, and the Americans had only two bazooka rounds left. At this point

US troops try to adapt to the demands of *bocage* fighting. Here a GI raises his helmet to draw German fire, although there is little evidence of his comrades being ready to reply if he is successful. A smashed MG 42 lies beside him. The photo may well have been posed for the cameraman. *(USNA)*

1/175th's radio problems were overcome, and the battalion called up three concentrations of defensive fire at 150 metres' distance, which dispersed the German assault groups. Lt Col Whiteford, who had been wounded earlier in the day, then relinquished command to Captain Miles Shorey, and 1/175th withdrew. Its positions were occupied by 3/175th Infantry, which in turn was relieved by 2/175th on 19 June. The relief took place in pouring rain, a suitable metaphor for the disappointment of the previous three days.

Gerhardt complained bitterly of his soldiers' alleged lack of aggression in these actions, but his exhortations were useless. The troops had suffered heavy losses and were now weary of the *bocage*. They were also very wary of the Germans, who were regarded as resolute, skilled and unpredictable.

Conversely, the Germans were much encouraged by their success; on 19 June they even launched some probing attacks, but made no real impact on 29th Division despite the American troops being tired and depleted. For example, 1/175th was reduced to only 12 officers and 308 men, having lost 22 officers and 502 men since 15 June. However, although unfit to attack, the US troops were capable of defence, and once they had been in place for a day it was almost impossible to shift them.

On 20 June Gerhardt insisted on making another assault on Villiers-Fossard, where the Germans held a salient jutting north between 115th and 175th Infantry. 1/115th and 3/115th, with some engineers and Sherman tanks in support, advanced on the village, but were stopped more than a kilometre from it. This was the final act of this phase of American attacks.

The arrival of German paratroops had a dramatic effect on the battle for St-Lô, shoring up Seventh Army's front and providing the Americans with their first combat experience against the *Wehrmacht*'s elite forces. *(BA 101I-586-2208-33A)*

29th Infantry Division was already conforming to the new First US Army policy of active defence for XIX Corps. The division adjusted its positions to create a defensible front line running from les Esserts (on the Vire north of la Germainerie), along the north bank of the Rau de la Jouenne via la Pégoterie, then to Hameau Secqueville, les Foulons and Couvains. GenLt Kraiss' forces reoccupied some ground, but left a no-man's-land up to 3 km deep. This was the arena for many skirmishes in the next few weeks as reconnaissance parties and raiding forces met and clashed. American activity was limited by the rationing of all supplies, particularly of artillery ammunition. The Germans took advantage of the lull. Battlegroup *Böhm* at Villiers-Fossard received 200 men from 30th

Mobile Brigade and three assault guns; Battlegroup *Goth* got five anti-tank guns. Other elements of 30th Mobile Brigade were placed in reserve and some of 352nd Division's artillery re-deployed to positions north-west of St-Lô. In an effort to deny information to the Americans, the French civilian population was also evacuated from an area extending 7 km south of the town.

A wounded American officer is evacuated from the battlefield. As this photo shows, the collection and movement of the wounded was greatly impeded by the *bocage*. (USNA)

By 25 June 352nd Division was reinforced with Battlegroup *Kentner* from 266th Infantry Division, consisting of most of 897th Grenadier Regiment and 11 artillery pieces, and the battered 914th Grenadier Regiment went into reserve. By 28 June another battlegroup, comprising 3rd Battalion, 898th Grenadiers (III/898th, from 343rd Infantry Division) had also arrived in 352nd Division's sector. *General* Meindl reported that II Paratroop Corps believed 'in its present position and with the units available, it is strong enough to face any enemy attack calmly'. On getting information about the effects of the great storm of 19–21 June, which badly interrupted Allied reinforcement and re-supply, GenLt Kraiss proposed a counter-attack led by 2nd SS Panzer Division *Das Reich* to throw back the American front. This was overruled; demands from other parts of Normandy had a higher priority. II Paratroop Corps' troops were told to improve their defences. Meanwhile, US XIX Corps reconstituted depleted rifle companies, studied the lessons of recent experiences and sent battalions to develop and learn new all-arms tactics for use in the *bocage*.

CHAPTER 3

OPERATIONS WEST OF THE VIRE, 8–20 JUNE

While US V Corps attacked east of the Vire, considerable effort was also devoted to establishing firm connections with Maj Gen J. Lawton Collins' VII Corps, advancing from Utah Beach. Much of the initial fighting involved 101st Airborne Division, which landed on D-Day. One of its main objectives was the capture of Carentan, 11 km west of Isigny. However, elements of 29th Division also played a part in the link-up, with 30th Infantry Division in the lead role west of the Vire as the Americans pushed towards St-Lô.

As described on p. 36, 175th Infantry Regiment entered Isigny early on 9 June. On the 10th Company K, 175th Infantry (K/175th) was ordered to seize the Vire crossing at Auville-sur-le-Vey (la Blanche on modern maps), 3 km west of Isigny. After its first attempt was repulsed the company tried again in the evening, assisted by a platoon from E/175th, some Shermans from 747th Tank Battalion, and 29th Reconnaissance Squadron's armoured cars.

> **Soldiers from K/175th described the action:**
>
> 'Jumped off about 1800. Engineers had made wooden rafts... sent Pvt Scott Roese (volunteer) out to see if he had to swim. He found river only up to his waist, so they decided not to use rafts. Tide was not in. Jumped off at left of bridge. No one on bridge, but machine guns were across river at right of bridge. One MG fired under bridge and hit Captain King... and killed [three] other men.

Captain King... dragged himself out of the water, refusing help, and directed his men across... Whole group crossed in 10 minutes. Two platoons crossed and firing stopped for a moment. The next two came over under cover of advanced platoons. Fired on creamery. One sniper was in tree nearby; everybody fired at him until he fell out. Moved forward to line of houses, shot into houses, went through town and up road to junction... We took up defence of the town and remained there, covering engineers who worked all night putting up bridge.'

Source: 'Interview of Company K, 175th Infantry Regiment', RG 407, Box 24014, Folder 81(i), USNA.

The Vire crossing at Auville-sur-le-Vey (la Blanche), looking west. K/175th Infantry waded across the river on the far side of the bridge. *(Tim Bean)*

On 11 June 29th Reconnaissance Squadron crossed the Vire and made contact with 101st Airborne Division near Catz, 2 km further west. Elements of 2nd Armored Division, which had begun landing on Omaha Beach two days earlier, also entered the area, reinforcing the junction between V and VII Corps. Simultaneously Maj Gen Collins' forces advanced towards Carentan from the north and east. After bitter fighting German troops abandoned the town and 101st Airborne Division moved in, securing Carentan by the evening of 12 June. Meanwhile 175th Infantry Regiment consolidated along

the east bank of the Vire, threatening crossings along a 10 km stretch of the river from Isigny in the north to Airel in the south.

352nd Infantry Division was aware of the link between V and VII Corps, and desperate to break it, but did not have the forces necessary. 17th SS Panzergrenadier Division was directed to Carentan on 10 June, but would not be fully assembled for two more days. LXXXIV Corps was overstretched, and in the crisis gave priority to the east over the west. 352nd Division was able to send only 250 men from I/914th Grenadiers west of the Vire, where they joined remnants of II/914th Grenadiers, IV/352nd Artillery Regiment and some anti-aircraft guns. GenLt Kraiss believed that the Americans could easily advance down the N174 to St-Lô, as there was little to stop them. However, on the evening of 11 June the first troops of Battlegroup *Heintz*, which had been badly delayed by Allied air attacks since leaving Brittany on 6 June, arrived. Commanded by *Oberst* Heintz, this battlegroup comprised the mobile elements of 275th Infantry Division, totalling around 4,100 men. Together with Engineer Battalion 'Angers', the battlegroup went into defensive positions along the Vire–Taute Canal, with combat outposts deployed towards the railway line running east from Carentan. To the left, the new arrivals were connected with 17th SS Panzergrenadier Division; on the right they joined up with the front held by 352nd Infantry Division along the Elle.

As the Germans were patching together their defences, on

Looking east towards the Vire from near Montmartin-en-Graignes. On 12 June E/175th Infantry crossed the river by the railway bridge on the left, before traversing the marshy area to the higher ground from which the picture was taken. *(ST)*

12 June the Americans attacked again. From the north, elements of 101st Airborne's 327th Glider Infantry Regiment (GIR) advanced down the N174 towards the Vire–Taute Canal. At the same time 175th Infantry sent C and E Companies west of the Vire to take the bridges carrying the D89 and N174 over the canal. Each company was to cross the river in assault boats provided by 121st Engineer Combat Battalion, E/175th Infantry next to the rail bridge, C/175th 1.5 km further south. They were to meet at Montmartin-en-Graignes, then proceed to their objectives. Unusually, Brig Gen Cota, 29th Division's assistant commander, accompanied E/175th.

Both companies got across the Vire, shielded from German fire by dykes on the banks. Once across, E/175th ran into an ambush in dense country near l'Enauderie, north-west of Montmartin. C/175th was also ambushed north of Montmartin, and scattered. The survivors of the companies met and combined, with a strength of 80 men, and tried to outflank the village to the east. However, they were stopped again and eventually dug in north-west of Montmartin, where they were joined by some men from 327th GIR. In the evening Cota led the force in a successful attack on the village, before moving to a nearby orchard for the night.

Maj Gen Gerhardt was displeased by the failure, reported by stragglers from E/175th. At 2300 hours G Company was sent across the river to capture the original objectives, accompanied by 175th Regiment's commander, Colonel Goode. During the night the company advanced 5 km south without a contact. By dawn G/175th was at la Raye, and moved north-west from there to high ground overlooking the N174 canal bridge. The company brought down

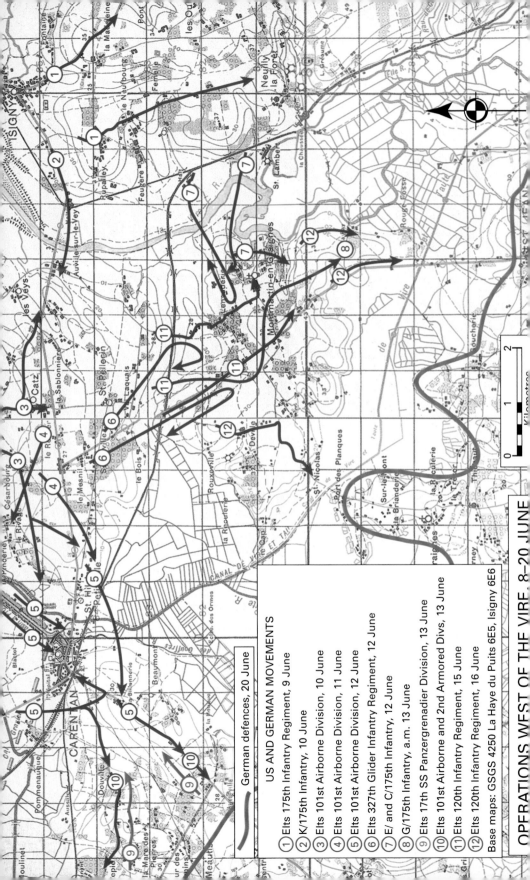

German defences, 20 June

US AND GERMAN MOVEMENTS

1. Elts 175th Infantry Regiment, 9 June
2. K/175th Infantry, 10 June
3. Elts 101st Airborne Division, 10 June
4. Elts 101st Airborne Division, 11 June
5. Elts 101st Airborne Division, 12 June
6. Elts 327th Glider Infantry Regiment, 12 June
7. E/ and C/175th Infantry, 12 June
8. G/175th Infantry, a.m. 13 June
9. Elts 17th SS Panzergrenadier Division, 13 June
10. Elts 101st Airborne and 2nd Armored Divs, 13 June
11. Elts 120th Infantry Regiment, 15 June
12. Elts 120th Infantry Regiment, 16 June

Base maps: GSGS 4250 La Haye du Puits 6E5, Isigny 6E6

OPERATIONS WEST OF THE VIRE, 8–20 JUNE

mortar and machine-gun fire on German transport on the road, which provoked a swift reaction.

Battlegroup *Heintz* retaliated with heavy fire of its own on G/175th, and then began to infiltrate the company's flanks. An assault followed, in which Captain John Slingluff, the officer commanding, was wounded. He ordered those who could to get out, just before the Germans made the final push preceded by showers of grenades. Thirty members of G/175th got back to US lines, but the rest were killed or captured. Slingluff and Colonel Goode were among those taken prisoner. Cota's group remained at Montmartin, too weak to attack but strong enough to defend.

Looking south-east along the Vire-Taute Canal from the bridge on the D89, one of 175th Infantry's objectives on 12 June. *(Author)*

At 1500 hours Gerhardt ordered his units to withdraw; 327th GIR also pulled back north of the railway. 352nd Infantry Division expected the Americans to reinforce and reported that there were too few troops between Montmartin and Airel to prevent a river crossing. But late on 13 June further elements of Battlegroup *Heintz* arrived and deployed just south of the railway. By the morning of 14 June LXXXIV Corps had blocked the easiest route to St-Lô, but still expected a strong attack on its forces astride the N174.

US actions on 12–13 June had been tentative and under-resourced. This was not surprising, since the Americans feared a major counter-offensive from the south to the area between Isigny and Carentan, which could separate the beachheads again. Their concerns were justified, for by the end of 12 June 17th SS Panzergrenadier Division and 6th Paratroop Regiment were assembled south-west of Carentan, ready to attack. During the morning of 13 June, however, the German assault was beaten off with heavy losses; officers in the two formations involved were astonished at the sheer volume of firepower they met, and began to lose their confidence in winning the war. Nevertheless, despite the Americans' defensive success, 17th SS Division's attack had the effect of focusing attention west of the inter-corps boundary. Instead of taking advantage of enemy weakness between the Taute and the Vire, on 14 June First US Army concentrated on pursuing the retreating Germans south-west of Carentan. East of Carentan no significant action took place on the 14th, and the Germans used the opportunity to improve their defences on the main route towards St-Lô.

Between 13 and 15 June a major re-organisation of US forces in Normandy took place. Slightly later than originally intended, at noon on 13 June Maj Gen Corlett's XIX Corps became operational, taking over the sector east of the Taute from VII Corps and deploying elements of its own 30th Infantry Division in the area. XIX Corps also assumed responsibility for the front east of the Vire as far as St-André-de-l'Épine, 6 km north-east of St-Lô. Since this was where 29th Infantry Division was already fighting, Gerhardt's men were transferred to Corlett's command on the 14th. On 15 June Maj Gen Troy H. Middleton's VIII Corps also entered the line, taking over command of 101st Airborne Division and, four days later, 82nd Airborne Division. Its role was to protect First Army's right flank between Carentan and the west coast, thus allowing VII Corps to focus on the advance to Cherbourg, the capture of which became its primary mission for the rest of the month.

On the afternoon of 14 June the inexperienced troops of 120th Infantry Regiment, from Maj Gen Leland Hobbs' 30th Infantry Division, moved into the area between the Vire and Taute rivers. Their instructions were to launch a limited attack to secure a defensible front along the Vire–Taute Canal. Patrols found the Germans posted in strongpoints around Montmartin. They also estimated that the terrain would favour the defenders, providing cover and good fields of fire. Accordingly 120th Regiment's commander, Colonel Hammond D. Birks, planned a set-piece assault. 3/120th and 2/120th were to attack from the Carentan–Bayeux railway, 3/120th astride the N174, heading for la Comté and 2/120th to the east, towards Montmartin-en-Graignes. Several artillery battalions, 743rd Tank Battalion and some tank-dozers

(Sherman tanks fitted with bulldozer blades) would be in support, with 1/120th in reserve. Battlegroup *Heintz* faced 120th Infantry, with its equally-inexperienced personnel in the sector where the battle was to take place.

Bicycles provided a valuable means of transport for the *Wehrmacht*, which was short of motor vehicles and fuel. These ones were abandoned during the battle for Montmartin-en-Graignes. *(USNA)*

Birks' men advanced at 0800 hours on 15 June, assisted by tanks and artillery. Lt Col Paul McCollom's 3/120th had one company on each side of the N174, with a third in reserve on the right. About 1 km beyond the railway, machine guns and 88s held up the attack until suppressed by 30th Division's artillery. 3/120th then pushed on to le Rata, delayed by mines on the road, snipers in trees and riflemen in the hedgerows. These positions were cleared using 60-mm mortars, rifle-grenades and BARs, while an outflanking move netted several prisoners and 'thirty good German bicycles'.

Further east, Lt Col William Bradford's 2/120th advanced astride the D444 in a mixed column of infantry and tanks, E Company leading. A patrol cleared hedges to the east along the flood plain. At l'Enauderie machine-gun fire forced the battalion to deploy on a wider front to find a clear way forward, but this manoeuvre was checked after a short distance by more strongpoints, deployed for mutual support. 1/120th was called forward by Colonel Birks, moving around the battlefield in his jeep, and a new plan was made.

A heavy machine gun, used to give sustained fire support, held in the fourth or weapons company of every battalion. Several men would be needed to serve the gun, to supply it with ammunition and water for the cooling jacket round the barrel. The soldier on the left has an M3 sub-machine gun. *(USNA)*

In the afternoon 2/120th attacked again. XIX Corps' historian recorded what happened next:

'Company F... pushed down the road to l'Enauderie, passing through a 300-yard gap in the American line to make an attack from the west of Montmartin, while Company E held astride the road. One platoon of Company F attacked from the south and the other from the west... Colonel Birks... saw that the tanks were not in action... and promptly threw them in to support, as one of Company F's platoons ran into a series of enemy dugouts and zigzag trenches in an orchard north of Montmartin. Seven tanks rolled in against the enemy dugouts, the tank-dozer shovelling dirt up against the entrances and the tanks piling them up. Company F then pushed in and occupied the town.'

Source: 'Montmartin-en-Graignes, 15–16 June 1944', 30th Division combat interviews, RG 407, Box 24037, Folder 94, USNA.

Meanwhile 3/120th resumed its own advance to clear la Comté by attacks from the north and north-west. This assault compromised the flank security of German units to the west, and they were ordered to fall back to the canal. By 1900 hours la Comté was secure, and patrols of 120th Infantry were on the north bank of the canal. However, Battlegroup *Heintz* still held a bridgehead north of the water on the N174, and observation posts beyond.

On 16 June two companies of 2/120th moved to la Raye, clearing hedgerows by flanking attacks, and dug in at an orchard west of the village. 3/120th mopped up German remnants north of the canal near the D89 bridge to the west. The Germans attempted a counter-attack, which was easily beaten off, and their observation posts were all pushed south of the canal.

The view south-west from near the Carentan–Isigny railway, showing the area attacked by 120th Infantry Regiment on 15 June. *(Author)*

Seventh Army expected that the success of 30th Infantry Division, which had gained an area roughly 4 km deep by 6 km wide, would be followed up at once by a major thrust along the N174. Instead, 30th Infantry Division settled down to consolidate defensive positions. It had secured the line of communication between the beachheads and the rear of the base for the attack on Cherbourg. For the moment its purpose was fulfilled.

On the German side Battlegroup *Heintz* kept a careful watch on its opponents, vigilant against reconnaissance and fighting patrols. On 18 June Seventh Army set up an artillery group near le Dézert, 6 km south of the Vire–Taute Canal, ready to provide fire support to the front line. Seventh Army remained convinced that the N174 offered its enemies an attractive avenue of attack south to St-Lô and beyond. However, the Americans had different priorities for the moment and further attacks in this sector would have to wait.

CHAPTER 4

RESUMPTION OF THE AMERICAN OFFENSIVE

There was no major action on the southern front until the end of June. First US Army was pre-occupied with capturing Cherbourg, while the Germans were compelled to give first priority to the sector between the Orne and the Drôme, where Second (British) Army launched strong attacks late in the month. This meant that II Paratroop Corps, holding a 26-km front east of the Vire, and LXXXIV Corps, defending the area between the Vire and the west coast of the Cotentin, lacked the resources necessary for decisive offensive action. Both sides used patrols and harassing artillery shoots to unsettle their enemies. Starting on 23 June, 2nd US Infantry Division began nightly 'serenades', limited to 20 shells a time, but targeting rest areas and field kitchens in particular. 3rd Paratroop Division regarded this as an uncivilised usage of war.

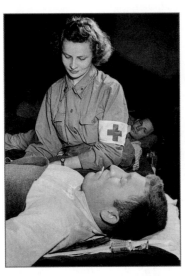

US troops wounded in Normandy could expect excellent medical care in field hospitals near the battlefield. Here Lieutenant Elizabeth Babarsik checks the temperature of Private John Bennett while other GIs look on, 5 July. *(USNA)*

Late in June both sides prepared for the resumption of operations west and east of St-Lô. Lt Gen Bradley planned to shift the entire First Army front forward, so that it ran in an almost straight line west from 1st Infantry Division's salient at Caumont. Once this was achieved, operations of a more decisive kind would be possible.

Bradley intended using several avenues of attack. Furthest west, VIII Corps was to turn the German left flank at Coutances, opening a route towards Brittany. The attack would be supported by VII Corps, redeployed from Cherbourg, pushing along the road from Carentan to Périers. East of the Taute, XIX Corps would advance astride the N174, regarded by Seventh Army as the best route to St-Lô. Corlett's forces would also attack east of the Vire, to eliminate the German position on Hill 122, north of St-Lô. This could be done by a direct assault after preliminary operations to clear outposts at le Carillon, Villiers-Fossard, and le Cauchais. The alternative was an indirect approach from the east, along the Martinville Ridge, menacing the rear of Hill 122. Success in this would require the seizure of Hill 192. To this end, V Corps' 2nd Infantry Division was also instructed to prepare an attack. If all went well, St-Lô and the critical high ground east and west of the town would fall into American hands, providing ideal jumping-off positions for the next phase of Bradley's offensive.

Villiers-Fossard, seen from the north, with the church tower towards the left. This was the area attacked by Task Force Y on 29 June. *(ST)*

On 29 June, as the last German resistance at Cherbourg was being mopped up, XIX Corps began a new attempt to reduce the salient at Villiers-Fossard, held by Battlegroup *Böhm*. The main effort was made by Maj Gen Leroy H. Watson's 3rd Armored Division, recently arrived in Normandy. Brig Gen Doyle O. Hickey's Combat Command A (CC A), comprising 32nd Armored Regiment,

A 3rd Armored Division Sherman, damaged near Villiers-Fossard. *(USNA)*

36th Armored Infantry Regiment and supporting arms, provided the strike force. Following consultation with XIX Corps about the nature of fighting in the *bocage*, CC A was divided into three task forces, X, Y and Z, each consisting of two assault groups and a reserve. The assault groups comprised a tank company, an infantry company, an engineer platoon and a platoon of tank destroyers apiece. Each also included two tank-dozers, which were to smash gaps in the hedgerows to facilitate the advance. Close co-operation between the various elements was demanded. Officers also studied maps and air photographs of the ground, although they knew little of the specific German positions or tactics.

At 0800 hours on the 29th US artillery and mortars began an hour of intense selective bombardments along the front from St-Georges-d'Elle to the Vire; fighter-bombers from US IX Tactical Air Command also attacked suspected German positions. CC A then moved forward, Task Force Y on the right, on both sides of Villiers-Fossard, and Task Force X on the left, east of the D6. Task Force Z remained in reserve along with 29th Division's 115th Infantry Regiment, which had been holding this sector for the previous week.

As the first shells landed, the soldiers of Battlegroup *Böhm* moved forward into the safety zone between the US troops and their own positions, depriving the preparatory bombardment of much of its effect. Consequently, when Colonel Parks' Task Force Y attacked, its progress was disrupted by improvised ambushes. The group on the right, under Lt Col Vincent Cockefair, was held up by infantry in the hedges and field corners, supported by four 88-mm guns. But Lt Col Nathaniel Whitlow's left-hand assault group advanced steadily, the infantry closely round the tanks to protect them from *Panzerfaust* teams. The Germans faded away after the third hedgerow, but mortar fire increased. The group silenced the mortars by calling up an artillery concentration onto the ridge at Villiers-Fossard. Concerned about his vulnerable right flank, Whitlow ordered his men to dig in just north of the creek at the base of the Villiers-Fossard ridge at 1100 hours. Later they crossed the stream, outflanked Villiers-Fossard and moved west into the sector of Cockefair's group, which took up positions behind them.

East of the D6, Colonel Truman E. Boudinot's Task Force X advanced methodically through the fields; tank-dozers forced the hedges, tanks then suppressed German defenders, while the infantry squads used fire and movement tactics to push forward. The group on the left (Lt Col Carlton Russell) soon reached the Bois de Bretel, on the D448. However, the right-hand group (Lt Col Walter Richardson) was delayed around la Fossardière. Accurate mortar fire also followed the US infantry until the German forward observer was spotted in a tree and killed. Blocked lines of sight made it difficult for this assault group to use its own fire support, but by 1300 hours it had reached the D448. Since Task Force Y was still north of Villiers-Fossard, Richardson placed a flank guard of some infantry and four tank destroyers near the D6. At 1500 hours Task Force X attacked again, paused to re-organize when stopped by a heavy mortar concentration, and then moved forward to an orchard west of Belle Fontaine. By 1900 hours Boudinot's men were close to their objective near la Luzerne, but were ordered to retire to the D448 because their right flank remained exposed.

The Germans fought hard on both sides of the D6, but could not hold the ground and were forced to retreat. In response, Seventh Army ordered 2nd SS Panzer Division to recall one of its battlegroups from the British sector, and to use it to reinforce the front north of St-Lô.

On the morning of 30 June CC A renewed the attack. Part of

Task Force Z was brought up and inserted in the line between the other assault groups. Task Force Y then moved forward, running into a German strongpoint at the creek north of le Bourg d'Enfer before outflanking it to the west. Meanwhile Task Force X advanced towards Belle Fontaine. Its left-hand group was engaged at a sunken lane north of the hamlet, and lost three Shermans. The right-hand group entered a long field south of the D448, where it was shelled by 88-mm guns located west of the D6 and ambushed by German infantry using short-range anti-tank weapons. Four Shermans were destroyed, and after a German counter-attack both groups of Task Force X fell back to the D448.

Having lost 411 men (including 60 killed) and 9 tanks destroyed, during the evening of 30 June CC A was relieved by 115th Infantry Regiment. By dusk, 29th Infantry Division held a line running south from la Pégoterie to Villiers-Fossard, then east via les Forges to just north of St-André-de-l'Épine. Seventh Army hoped to relieve 352nd Infantry Division with elements of 243rd and 266th Infantry Divisions, and to concentrate 2nd SS Panzer Division as a reserve against further attacks. The Germans were convinced that the fall of Cherbourg would be followed swiftly by stronger attacks on St-Lô. But, for the next week, US troops east of the Vire reverted to active defence whilst preparing to deploy the newly arrived 35th Infantry Division on their western flank.

XIX CORPS ATTACKS

On 3 July Maj Gen Middleton's VIII Corps launched First Army's offensive near the west coast of the Cotentin, joined the next day by VII Corps. German units fought doggedly to stop the American advance. US casualties were heavy and, although gains were made and Seventh Army's reserves were drawn into battle, overall progress was slow. Within a few days it became clear that any hope that a swift penetration west of St-Lô would cause the Germans to abandon the town were likely to be frustrated. If XIX Corps was to capture its objectives, it would have to do so in battle.

Maj Gen Corlett's plan, as contained in XIX Corps Field Order No. 4 of 2 July, was for a two-phase attack. The initial assault would involve 30th Infantry Division, part of which was to cross the Vire–Taute Canal and drive south along the N174. The rest of the division was to attack from the east, crossing the Vire near St-Fromond before thrusting towards St-Lô. When Pont-Hébert, 6 km north of St-Lô, was reached, the assault would begin in the eastern part of XIX Corps' sector, carried out by 29th Infantry Division. V Corps' 2nd Infantry Division was also to join the attack, while Corlett would commit 35th Infantry Division according to need. 3rd Armored Division, located east of the Vire, was available for exploitation; however, as a First Army reserve, this would depend on Bradley's instructions.

US artillerymen send a personal message to the *Führer*, 4 July 1944. The photograph was taken near Couvains, in 29th Division's sector. *(USNA)*

On 7 July 30th Division began its attack. The immediate objective was the crossroads at le Fleurion, on the N174 south of St-Jean-de-Daye, and the high ground to the east. The intention was to exploit south to Point 91 (les Hauts Vents) and to Pont-Hébert. The plan was for Colonel Henry Kelly's 117th Infantry to cross the Vire near St-Fromond at 0430 hours, supported and followed by 119th Infantry. At 1330 hours, once the Germans had been drawn to St-Fromond, 120th Infantry would cross the Vire–Taute Canal. It would then advance south, meeting 117th Infantry at le Fleurion before continuing the attack towards Pont-Hébert.

The US offensive was given powerful artillery support, although owing to bad weather the intended air bombardment was cancelled. At 0330 hours, nine battalions of corps artillery fired on known and suspected German gun positions. They were joined at 0415 by 30th Division's artillery, together with the 4.2-inch mortars of 92nd Chemical Battalion and the guns of 823rd Tank Destroyer Battalion,

HISTORY

Base maps: GSGS 4250
6F1/5F2 Periers, 6F2 St-Lô

─────	Front line, end 7 July
─-─-─	Front line, end 8 July
┈┈┈┈	Front line, end 9 July
━━━━	Front line, end 10 July

Supporting elements, including tank, tank destroyer, reconnaissance, artillery and other units, are not shown. Units in reserve west of the Vire are also not shown. See also Tour Map B on page 136.

US MOVEMENTS
AND POSITIONS

1 1/117th Infantry
2 2/117th Infantry
3 3/117th Infantry
4 1/119th Infantry
5 2/119th Infantry
6 3/119th Infantry
7 1/120th Infantry
8 2/120th Infantry
9 3/120th Infantry
10 Elts 3rd Armd Div
11 Elts 113th Cav Gp
12 1/39th Infantry
13 2/39th Infantry
14 3/39th Infantry
15 1/47th Infantry
16 2/47th Infantry
17 3/47th Infantry
18 1/60th Infantry
19 2/60th Infantry
20 3/60th Infantry

0   1   2
Kilometres

XIX CORPS' OFFENSIVE, 7–10 JULY

firing at the German front line. As 117th Infantry moved forward, the artillery and mortars delivered a rolling barrage, 270 metres ahead. However, despite instructions to 'hug' the bombardment as it advanced 90 metres every five minutes, the infantry were unable to keep up. Consequently, the barrage was stopped soon after the attack began, and the operation proceeded without it.

Soon after 0430 hours, 32 boat parties of Lt Col Arthur Fuller's 2/117th Infantry, each of twelve men, started to cross the Vire near St-Fromond. E/117th was on the right and F/117th on the left. G/117th followed F Company at H+10 minutes. The crossing was north of a bend in the river, to deprive machine guns at the St-Fromond bridge of a line of sight. The river here was 20 metres wide, the battalion on a front of 365 metres.

Fuller's men had practised intensively for the assault, and were rewarded for their preparation. Using scaling ladders to get over the embankment west of the river, they moved quickly across 350 metres of open ground to the first hedge. They were engaged by machine guns and artillery, and by 0445 hours German guns and mortars were shooting at the river and its banks. E/ and F/117th advanced despite this, each with two platoons forward, and their light automatic weapons concentrated on their flanks. The two companies reached the D8, then swung right astride the road towards le Fleurion. Meanwhile, G/117th moved up behind them to clear St-Fromond.

By 0800 hours St-Fromond had been swept. G/117th, with platoons of H/117th (the weapons company) then advanced west behind the leading troops. By 1430 hours 2/117th was near la Touperrie, 400 metres east of le Fleurion, but was aware of Germans moving on its flanks, so stopped and dug in for all-round defence. Later that night five tanks and some infantry counter-attacked the American position, but were beaten off.

Back in St-Fromond, 30th Division engineers worked frantically under artillery fire to bridge the River Vire. Despite numerous casualties, by 0600 hours they had constructed a footbridge, and by three hours later had repaired the road bridge so it could bear the weight of tanks. Two pontoon bridges followed. Using these facilities, 3/117th crossed the river and advanced north-west to occupy Hill 30 (Point 44 on modern maps) east of St-Jean-de-Daye. 1/117th followed, and dug in south of the D8. At 1015 hours 2/119th Infantry Regiment and 743rd Tank Battalion began crossing the river, followed by 823rd Tank Destroyer Battalion.

US infantry and a tank-dozer cross the bridge at St-Fromond. The role of American engineers in repairing this bridge, and in constructing vehicle and foot bridges nearby, was critical to XIX Corps' success on 7 July. *(USNA)*

These elements moved south of the D8, but were checked by panzers and anti-tank guns near the abbey 1 km to the south-west.

To the north, Colonel Birks' 120th Infantry Regiment crossed the Vire–Taute Canal during the afternoon of 7 July, 1/120th east of the N174, 3/120th to the west, with 2/120th providing a flank guard north of the waterway. 3/120th was delayed by a mis-calculation about the length of floating bridges required, but 1/120th waded across the canal, attracting heavy fire from the Germans on the slopes ahead. Nevertheless the Americans pressed on and penetrated Battlegroup *Heintz*'s defences. Despite further delays caused by German artillery, 3/120th caught up, and the two battalions by-passed St-Jean-de-Daye. By nightfall Birks' men were in positions west of St-Jean-de-Daye, and had linked up with 3/117th to their left. The Americans then dug in, ready to resume the advance the next morning.

Battlegroup *Heintz* could not cope with the onslaught, and Seventh Army was compelled to take immediate measures to prevent a collapse. Rejecting protests from *General* Meindl that his forces were over-stretched, II Paratroop Corps was told to send 30th Mobile Brigade and its last uncommitted battalion west of the Vire. Army Group B also intervened, ordering the assembly of the Panzer Lehr Division, just withdrawn from opposite the British front in an attempt to create a reserve, between Périers and St-Lô. From here, Panzer Lehr was to support 17th SS Panzergrenadier Division, which was responsible for the front west of the Vire. Elements of 2nd SS Panzer Division were also to re-deploy, with the aim of halting further penetrations by the American forces.

Lt Gen Bradley was also impressed by 30th Division's success. During the afternoon of 7 July he decided that Maj Gen Watson's 3rd Armored Division should be placed under XIX Corps for exploitation purposes. However, although Bradley appears to have envisaged a relatively limited initial commitment, Maj Gen Corlett decided to launch a more ambitious attack against what he perceived as disintegrating German resistance. At 1900 hours he issued XIX Corps Field Order No. 5, ordering 3rd Armored to begin a 'powerdrive' towards the high ground west of St-Lô. To this end, Maj Gen Hobbs' 30th Infantry Division was to clear the route from St-Fromond to le Fleurion, allowing Watson's two combat commands to drive west without interruption. The armour was then to swing left, attacking down the N174 towards St-Lô. Hobbs' troops were to follow rapidly in support.

However, the American plan quickly unravelled. When his subordinates reported that their battalions were dispersed and out of contact with one another, Hobbs decided not to order them to press on to capture le Fleurion. Additionally, owing to the destruction of one of the pontoon bridges at St-Fromond by German artillery, considerable congestion developed along the D8. When the first elements of 3rd Armored Division's CC B, under the command of Brig Gen John Bohn, crossed the Vire at about 1900 hours, they became stuck in a traffic jam. Although the leading task force (X, under Lt Col Cockefair) established itself on the west bank, it ran into significant opposition near St-Fromond Abbey. This added to the overall impression of an insecure bridgehead, and encouraged Bohn to wait until the following morning before beginning his attack.

Even more significantly, Maj Gen Watson had already decided

on a route of advance different to that indicated in XIX Corps' subsequent Field Order No. 5. Watson feared that an advance along the N174 would expose his forces to counter-attack from the west. Consequently, his instructions to Bohn were to move south across country as soon as CC B crossed the river, and to join the N174 near Pont-Hébert. Although a copy of Watson's order was passed to 30th Division's headquarters, there was insufficient time to co-ordinate plans. As a result, when the Americans resumed their advance, CC B and Colonel Alfred Ednie's 119th Infantry Regiment found themselves trying to attack from the same congested bridgehead and through the same difficult terrain. This was a recipe for confusion and a significant loss of momentum.

Traffic chaos near St-Fromond. The decision to send 3rd Armored Division's Combat Command B to exploit 30th Infantry Division's success overloaded the local road net, causing confusion and delay. *(USNA)*

During the night of 7–8 July, Colonel William Biddle's 113th Cavalry Group (113th and 125th Cavalry Squadrons) crossed the Vire–Taute Canal behind 120th Infantry Regiment, and then wheeled south-west. Its role was to screen 30th Division's advance on the right by destroying German forces around Graignes. It was also to maintain contact with US VII Corps, advancing along the west bank of the River Taute. However, although la Goucherie and le Mesnil-Véneron fell to the Americans, attempts to push further west were stopped by 38th SS Panzergrenadier Regiment (from 17th SS Panzergrenadier Division). Concerned that a counter-stroke could uncover 30th Division's rear as it pushed south, Biddle ordered his troops to switch to the defensive. By 1600 hours this was being done, although 125th Cavalry Squadron also managed to establish contact with 3/120th on its left flank. This battalion fought throughout 8 July to secure the high ground north of le Dézert, which it achieved after repulsing a counter-attack. Meanwhile, 1/120th and 3/117th cleared le Fleurion and advanced to les Osmonds (la Perrine on modern maps). During the afternoon, 2/120th crossed the canal and advanced south. By early the next morning it was ready to lead the attack towards St-Lô west of the N174. 3rd Armored Division's CC A also entered the bridgehead at St-Fromond, moving with difficulty along the crowded D8, to support 113th Cavalry Group at la Goucherie.

Three Germans lie dead near St-Fromond, victims of 30th Infantry Division's attack on 7 July. *(USNA)*

Early on 8 July, Task Force X attempted to move south from St-Fromond. After knocking out four Panzer IVs at the abbey, the battlegroup moved slowly from field to field (movement along the narrow roads was avoided for fear of ambush). However, when elements of the task force exchanged shots with 119th Infantry

Regiment, it became apparent that 30th Infantry Division's units were unaware of the plan to use CC B in the same area. For this reason, at 1500 hours Brig Gen Bohn convened a meeting with officers of 30th Infantry Division to co-ordinate future action. Later that afternoon, Task Force X reached la Bernardrie, north-west of Cavigny, and halted to refuel and repair its vehicles. 119th Infantry also advanced from St-Fromond, and by nightfall was on the heights north of Cavigny, level with Task Force X. At 2200 hours Maj Gen Corlett attached CC B to 30th Division, to prevent further confusion when the attack resumed the next day.

A tank-dozer smashes through a Normandy hedgerow. Vehicles like this were also used to bury German tunnel systems and for various engineer tasks. *(USNA)*

Despite the Americans' difficulties, 8 July was a day of further concern for Seventh Army. Although 30th Mobile Brigade and 12th Paratroop Reconnaissance Battalion arrived west of the Vire and launched a few counter-attacks, they achieved little. Nevertheless, the Germans had some reason for optimism. Having received permission to move 5th Paratroop Division from Brittany to Normandy, Seventh Army intended withdrawing 2nd SS Panzer Division and concentrating it west of the Taute, ready to intervene on the boundary between US VII and XIX Corps. More significantly, Panzer Lehr Division was placed under LXXXIV Corps, with instructions to eliminate the Vire bridgehead by a counter-attack. However, this could not take place for at least two days. In the meantime, as LXXXIV Corps' commander, now GenLt Dietrich von Choltitz, informed Seventh Army's Chief of Staff at 2330 hours on the 8th, 9 July was likely to be 'a critical day'.

VII CORPS ENTERS THE BATTLE

On 8 July, in a decision that would have considerable influence on the battle for St-Lô, Maj Gen Collins secured Lt Gen Bradley's agreement to the deployment of VII Corps' 9th Infantry Division east of the Taute. Up to this point, VII Corps had struggled to advance astride the Carentan–Périers road, and had suffered severe losses trying to press home its attacks. By extending its sector across the Taute, Collins hoped to outflank German resistance from the east. Furthermore, although XIX Corps would lose some of its own room for manoeuvre, it would gain considerably in terms of right flank security. Given that air reconnaissance was revealing the imminent arrival of powerful German reserves west of the Vire, 9th Infantry Division's deployment was also welcome for the extra combat power that it represented. Even though there was no intention of using it to repel Panzer Lehr's planned counter-attack – the details of which were unknown to the Americans – barely 36 hours after its arrival south of the Vire–Taute Canal, it would play a critical role in doing precisely that.

At 0200 hours on 9 July, 30th Division headquarters issued Field Order No. 4, outlining the forthcoming day's operations. An advance of roughly 4 km was demanded, with CC B leading the attack to Point 91 (les Hauts Vents). This important terrain feature was about 1.5 km west of Pont-Hébert, at the northern end of a long ridgeline between the Vire and Terette rivers. Hobbs' infantry regiments would follow: 120th Infantry with 743rd Tank Battalion in the west; 117th Infantry astride the N174; and 119th Infantry in the east. Pending the arrival of 9th Infantry Division, 113th Cavalry Group and CC A would cover the front between la Goucherie and le Dézert. Reflecting growing concerns about counter-attacks, 823rd Tank Destroyer Battalion would remain at le Fleurion, to deal with any German penetration northwards along the highway. On Corlett's suggestion, anti-tank weapons were posted well forward, while US artillery was instructed to respond immediately to calls for assistance from units under attack.

2/120th advanced at 1000 hours, but was held up by a strong-point on Hill 32 (shown on modern maps as Point 28, near les Landes), south-east of le Dézert. In the hedgerows, the battalion soon lost contact with 3/117th on its left. At 1230 hours elements of a newly arrived battlegroup from 2nd SS Panzer Division counter-attacked, and by 1510 hours German infantry supported by some Panzer IVs had got between 2/120th and 3/117th Infantry. Simultaneously B/743rd Tank Battalion was lured into an ambush and lost a dozen Shermans. 2/120th fell back 400 metres and organised an all-round defence. The 2nd SS Panzer Division troops, mostly from the engineer battalion, moved north to attack 1/120th, supported by around four battalions of artillery. However, 120th Infantry called for indirect fire support, and within an hour no fewer than 18 battalions of guns were being used to place protective box barrages around Colonel Birks' forces. According to Seventh Army's war diary, 2nd SS Panzer Division's counter-attack 'disintegrated' under this fire, and by dusk the 120th's sector was stable, with its three battalions dug in south-east of le Dézert.

An American M12 155-mm self-propelled gun in action. Note the camouflage net, to screen the gun from German observers. *(USNA)*

Meanwhile, 117th Infantry advanced with its 1st Battalion east of the N174, 3rd Battalion west of the highway, and 2/117th in reserve. Satisfactory progress was made, but aerial reconnaissance reports started arriving of an armoured thrust northwards along the main road. In scenes of considerable confusion during the afternoon, some of 117th's troops panicked and fled. They were joined by over a hundred soldiers from 823rd Tank Destroyer

A Sherman tank moves past two knocked out Panzer IVs, possibly from 2nd SS Panzer Division, on 9 July. *(USNA)*

Battalion and 30th Division's anti-aircraft units. However, the German counter-attack proved illusory and order was rapidly restored. By nightfall the regiment's forward elements were in position near the Château de la Mare, 1.5 km south of la Perrine.

East of the N174, 119th Infantry and CC B were both trying to advance quickly, and getting in each other's way. In the morning Colonel Graeme Parks' Task Force Y passed through Task Force X at la Bernardrie and took up the lead, with Task Force Z (Lt Col Samuel Hogan) advancing on its right. But despite ineffective resistance the Americans' cross-country movement was slow, and Maj Gen Hobbs told Bohn that unless he reached Point 91 by 1700 hours, he would be relieved. Bohn went forward, ordering his subordinates to use minor roads and lanes to expedite their advance. This proved successful, but when I/33rd Armored Regiment reached the N174 at 1630 hours it mistakenly turned north. Within minutes it ran into 30th Division's 90-mm anti-aircraft guns, deployed in the anti-tank role, and lost two Shermans to 'friendly fire' (this incident may have ignited the panic described above). The column turned south, and by dusk both task forces were on the high ground 1 km north of Pont-Hébert, with H/33rd Armored Regiment in the town itself. A few tanks pressed on towards Point 91, but lost radio contact and were isolated. At this stage CC B received new orders to halt and defend the ridge north of Pont-Hébert. Although Bohn asked for permission to continue the advance, Hobbs was concerned about the unit's open right flank, and refused. The task forces recalled most of their leading elements and re-organized. Brig Gen Bohn was then summoned to 30th Division headquarters, where he was sacked by Maj Gen Hobbs. Colonel Dorrance S. Roysdon took over CC B for the next day's operations.

Seventh Army had enjoyed some defensive success on 9 July, and its war diary entry described the situation west of the Vire as being 'not considered serious'. However, although limited counter-attacks might check and delay XIX Corps' advance, the US assault could not be stopped with the available forces. The only hope for a significant improvement lay in a successful counter-stroke by Panzer Lehr Division, which was planned to take place the following day.

On 10 July the Americans advanced again, and in greater numbers. Having crossed the Vire–Taute Canal the previous evening, 9th Infantry Division fanned out towards the Taute. 60th Infantry Regiment, supported by 113th Cavalry Group, went west through la Goucherie to the outskirts of Graignes; 47th Infantry Regiment deployed left of the 60th, reaching a point just east of the Bois du Hommet. 39th Infantry Regiment, however, advanced more slowly astride the D8, and only secured le Dézert late in the day. As a result it lost contact with 47th Infantry on its right, which unsuccessfully tried to cover the 1,600-metre gap between them with a single rifle company from the regiment's 3rd Battalion.

30th Infantry Division also attacked on 10 July, but with just 119th and 120th Infantry Regiments forward, because the divisional front had been reduced. South of 9th Division's sector, 3/120th advanced via Hill 32 to le Rocher, 1 km north of Point 91. 1/120th followed up, with 2/120th watching the western flank. Meanwhile, east of the N174, 2/119th set off at 0700 hours from near Cavigny, joined two hours later by 3/119th, which had been delayed by a shortage of ammunition. By 1030 hours they were closing in on Pont-Hébert from the north-east, but were obstructed by the tanks of CC B, manoeuvring on the high ground to their right.

In the centre, CC B was ordered at 0200 hours on the 10th to prepare to resume its attack towards Point 91. Four hours later it moved off, led by Task Force X, pushing along a sunken road (now the D377) towards les Hauts Vents. German resistance was determined, and knocked out tanks frequently blocked the road. Attempts to move cross-country encountered heavy anti-tank fire, and eventually the advance stalled 700 metres from Point 91, in the area held by 3/120th Infantry. Later Task Force Z moved forward to reinforce the assault, but was stopped by gunfire from Belle-Lande (shown on 1944 maps, but now incorporated in the northern outskirts of Pont-Hébert).

An infantry squad advances down a road, while other men carefully examine the hedgerow. Often small pockets of Germans stragglers emerged from hidden dug-outs to fire on the rear of American troops on the advance. *(USNA)*

In an attempt to co-ordinate plans more closely, at 1535 hours the commanders of 30th Infantry and 3rd Armored Divisions held a conference, also attended by Colonel Alfred V. Ednie (119th Infantry) and Colonel Roysdon (CC B). As a result, it was decided to use 119th Infantry to outflank Point 91 from the east. At 1830 hours 3/119th was ordered to advance through Belle-Lande to la Fautelaye, on the ridge 1 km south of les Hauts Vents. 2/119th, joined by 1/119th, would advance along the Vire, capturing Pont-Hébert and the river ford 750 metres further south at la Bessinière. However, when Ednie's troops attacked, they were stopped almost immediately by dug-in tanks and infantry at Belle-Lande. Some of the resistance appears to have come from remnants of Battlegroup *Heintz*. However, the tanks were almost certainly part of the Panzer Lehr Division, elements of which had been arriving throughout the day from the direction of St-Lô.

Asleep with a buddy and overhead cover. Two infantrymen in a well-protected foxhole, with a supply of grenades ready to hand to repel attackers. *(USNA)*

The advance was beginning to lose momentum, though Corlett was sure that one more strong effort would bring decisive success and that LXXXIV Corps was close to collapse. Hobbs was less sanguine; in a phone conversation at 1750 hours he said: 'The 30th has its neck stuck out.' The Germans were firing into the division's left flank from across the Vire; on the right 9th Infantry Division was only at le Dézert, and the vehicles of CC B were still getting in the way of his troops. At 1950 hours Corlett ordered Hobbs to carry on a vigorous offensive on 11 July. However, on 11 July it was the Germans who seized the initiative and launched the strongest counter-attack they would make in the battle for St-Lô.

HISTORY

CHAPTER 5

11 JULY: THE CRITICAL DAY

On the evening of 10 July, GenLt Fritz Bayerlein's Panzer Lehr Division took over the sector of Battlegroup *Heintz* west of the Vire. This division, though it was formidably manned by instructors in armoured warfare, had suffered badly in its earlier fighting against the British, and only a hundred of its original 232 tanks and assault guns were serviceable. Nevertheless, following a meeting with

SS-Oberstgruppenführer Paul Hausser, Seventh Army's commander, Bayerlein planned to attack on 11 July. In the west 901st Panzer-grenadier Regiment, plus some 30 Panther tanks, was to advance from le Hommet-d'Arthenay towards St-Jean-de-Daye. In the east, a battlegroup based on 902nd Panzergrenadier Regiment would attack from Pont-Hébert to St-Fromond. To evade American tactical aircraft, the attack was to start at night. The Germans hoped that by the time daylight arrived, their two battlegroups would be so intermingled with their opponents that the Americans would be unable to use their air power and artillery. If all went well, within 24 hours the bridgehead south of the Vire–Taute Canal would be eradicated, removing the most direct threat to St-Lô and freeing German forces for use elsewhere.

Order of Battle Panzer Lehr Division
11 July 1944
(principal units only)

Commander	*Generalleutnant Fritz Bayerlein*
130th Panzer Demonstration Regt	*Oberst Rudolf Gerhardt*
II/130th Panzer Demonstration Regt	*Major Helmut Ritgen*
I/6th Panzer Regt (attached)	*Major Markowski*
901st Panzergrenadier Demonstration Regt	*Oberst Georg Scholze*
I/901st Panzergrenadier Demonstration Regt	*Hauptmann Karl Philipps*
II/901st Panzergrenadier Demonstration Regt	*Major Schöne*
902nd Panzergrenadier Demonstration Regt	*Oberstleutnant Welsch*
I/902nd Panzergrenadier Demonstration Regt	*Major Kuhnow*
II/902nd Panzergrenadier Demonstration Regt	*Hauptmann K. Böhm*
130th Panzer Demonstration Recce Btn	*Hauptmann H. Hübner*
130th Panzer Demonstration Anti-Tank Btn	*Major Joachim Barth*
130th Panzer Artillery Regiment (three btns)	*Major Zeisler*
130th Panzer Engineer Battalion	*Major W. Brandt*
311th Army Anti-Aircraft Battalion	*Hauptmann Weinkopf*

Attached units:
Battlegroup *Wisliceny* (reinforced I/3rd SS Panzergrenadier Regiment); 12th Paratroop Reconnaissance Battalion; Battlegroup *Heintz* (see p. 23); 628th Heavy Artillery Battalion

Note: 6th Company, II/130th Panzer Regiment and one company from the anti-tank battalion, plus other divisional elements, were still opposing British troops on 11 July. Owing to losses sustained in earlier fighting, few combat units (apart from the artillery) were at much more than 50 per cent of original strength on 11 July.

Panzer Lehr's movement from the British to the American sector had been monitored by Allied signals intelligence, and a message warning of its intentions was sent to 21st Army Group on 10 July.

HISTORY

Unlike the Panzer Lehr's knocked-out tanks, US vehicles damaged on 11 July could be recovered and quickly put back into action. Here a Sherman is towed to a repair facility near le Dézert. *(USNA)*

However, although XIX Corps was aware of a possible counter-blow, front-line units received no specific information about Panzer Lehr's plans. Consequently, when the Germans attacked, they achieved tactical surprise. Unfortunately for them, against the multi-layered defences presented by their opponents, this proved insufficient to bring them anywhere near the success they desired.

As described in Tour B (*pp. 135–50*), Panzer Lehr began its advance very early on 11 July. In the west, 901st Panzergrenadiers burst through a gap in 9th Infantry Division's lines, overrunning a battalion headquarters and threatening to fragment the US forces. Meanwhile, part of the 902nd Panzergrenadiers' battlegroup infiltrated 119th Infantry Regiment's positions and advanced towards Cavigny. West of Pont-Hébert the rest of 902nd Panzergrenadiers, supported by some Panzer IVs, advanced north from Point 91, getting within a few metres of 3/120th Infantry's command post at le Rocher before the alarm was sounded.

As soon as the Americans realised what was happening, however, they fought back with determination. A critical role was played by 899th Tank Destroyer Battalion, which held a number of road junctions behind the US front. Although no match for Panzer Lehr's Panthers in a straight fight, in the *bocage* at night its M10s could ambush the German armour at close range. When the leading panzers ran into these positions and were destroyed, several avenues of attack became blocked. By daylight VII Corps and XIX Corps were fully alert to the threat posed by Bayerlein's troops, and reacted swiftly to seal possible routes of penetration and to cut off German lines of retreat. Infantry and armoured reserves were committed, and squadrons of P-47 Thunderbolts swooped down to strafe and bomb the German columns. North of Pont-Hébert, elements of CC B re-deployed against 902nd Panzergrenadiers and its supporting armour. By midday, with the exception of a few desperate thrusts west of le Dézert, Panzer Lehr's attack had run out of steam. Nowhere had it penetrated to within 3 km of the bridges at St-Fromond, or within sight of the Vire–Taute Canal.

As the German assault lost momentum, American troops tried to implement Corlett's instructions from the previous day. In fierce hedgerow fighting, 30th Division's 120th Infantry Regiment advanced on both sides of the D377 past le Rocher. East of the N174, 119th Infantry closed in on Pont-Hébert. The greatest success, however, was recorded by CC B. Despite losses to dug-in German tanks and to artillery fire, during the late afternoon Task Forces Z and X drove onto the northern end of the ridge at les Hauts Vents. 2/120th pushed up in support and dug in on the forward slopes, with the tanks and armoured infantry nearby. Task Force Z was now able to see across an extensive swathe of country to the south and west, although it also found itself exposed to two days of intense and demoralising bombardment.

11 July was a decisive day for LXXXIV Corps, which faced the double blow of further American advances west of the Taute and the failure of the strongest attack so far mounted by its own forces. Panzer Lehr Division had temporarily gained some ground, but could not break through, and had lost over 700 men and around 30 tanks trying to do so. The US troops were too numerous, skilled and resolute. The presence of VII Corps' 9th Infantry Division came as a surprise to LXXXIV Corps, which concluded that its attack had run into a simultaneous offensive by US forces. Reacting to this renewed threat to St-Lô, at 2245 hours Hausser informed Army

Group B that he intended deploying 5th Paratroop Division behind Panzer Lehr as soon as it arrived. Yet news now came from east of the Vire which appeared to call into question the relevance of further defensive measures west of the river. The Americans had broken II Paratroop Corps' month-long hold on Hill 192, and were advancing along the Martinville Ridge towards St-Lô from the north-east.

A Panzer Lehr Division Panther allegedly knocked out by a bazooka near le Dézert on 11 July. *(USNA)*

THE APPROACH TO ST-LÔ

In accordance with his original plan, on 11 July Corlett's Corps extended its offensive to the area east of the Vire. Here, Maj Gen Paul Baade's 35th Infantry Division had deployed in the sector held by 175th Infantry Regiment on 9–10 July. This allowed 29th Division to shorten its front from 8 km to 4 km, and to put 175th Infantry into reserve. The XIX Corps plan for 11 July was to attack all along the front; 29th Infantry Division was to drive onto the eastern end of the Martinville Ridge before swinging westwards behind Hill 122, while Baade's troops would push south into the loop of the River Vire between Pont-Hébert and St-Lô. This would assist 30th Infantry Division's advance by threatening Panzer Lehr Division's right flank. Simultaneously, on 29th Division's left, US V Corps was to unleash a hurricane of fire onto Hill 192, prior to launching an assault on this critical feature. If successful, this would secure XIX Corps' left flank while the latter drove south. With the Germans under pressure along their entire front, US commanders hoped they would abandon St-Lô, allowing the Americans to seize the town and the high ground west and east of it.

Facing the US assault was *General* Meindl's II Paratroop Corps. East of the D6, including Hill 192 and the area beyond, were parts of 3rd Paratroop Division, principally 9th Paratroop Regiment. West of them were the remnants of 352nd Infantry Division, including attached battlegroups. Battlegroup *Böhm* was astride the D6, with 916th Grenadiers on its left. Most of the soldiers facing US 35th Infantry Division, however, came from Battlegroups *Rambach* and *Kentner* (*see p. 22*). They held a string of positions from la Meauffe southwards, notably a superbly laid-out strongpoint near the hamlet of le Carillon, at the northern end of the ridge running south-east to Hill 122.

35th Infantry Division deployed with two regiments forward: 137th in the west, along the Vire, and 320th in the east. 134th Infantry Regiment was in corps reserve. According to orders issued on 10 July, both regiments were to advance south-west, halting in the Vire loop 5 km away. However, the American troops were inexperienced, with little understanding of the realities of fighting in the *bocage*. Nor were they particularly well informed about the enemy, or about the position at le Carillon. Some poor weather also precluded direct air support, although the division was assisted by armour and artillery, and entered the battle with high morale.

35th Infantry Division attacked at 0600 hours, but made little progress against well-organised opposition. Colonel Bernard Byrne's 320th Infantry approached le Carillon, but was stopped by the defences. Meanwhile 137th Infantry secured la Meauffe (la Germainerie on modern maps) and advanced towards St-Gilles. But the regiment's commander, Colonel Grant Layng, was wounded, and the attack stalled in the face of heavy machine-gun, mortar and artillery fire. At the end of the day St-Gilles remained in German hands, leaving 137th Infantry a kilometre short of 30th Infantry Division's front line west of the Vire. This had a detrimental effect on 30th Division's attempts to advance into Pont-Hébert, which continued to be exposed to German fire from beyond the river.

Further east, 29th Infantry Division's plan for 11 July was to attack in two areas. On the right, 115th Infantry Regiment would advance on a wide front astride the D6, pinning the Germans and capturing le Bourg d'Enfer, Belle Fontaine and la Luzerne. Further east, 116th Infantry was to make the decisive attack, led by its 2nd Battalion. This unit was to penetrate 3rd Paratroop Division's line at St-André-de-l'Épine, followed by the rest of the regiment. 3/116th would seek to capture a position astride the D972 highway at la Boulaye, before attacking towards St-Lô. Immediately to the north, 2/116th and 1/116th would advance west along the parallel Martinville Ridge. 175th Regiment would be available to reinforce. Familiar with the problems of the *bocage*, 29th Infantry Division had rehearsed its all-arms tactics carefully. Its infantry squads were well supported by tanks and engineers, and by the ubiquitous and capable US artillery.

However, the Germans moved first. Following an intense bombardment of the US front throughout 10 July, at 0130 hours on the 11th a German battlegroup raided the positions held by 1/115th. The Germans, from II/9th Paratroop Regiment, pushed up the creek at Belle Fontaine and infiltrated between 3/115th and Major Glover Johns' 1/115th. Supported by a rolling barrage, they overran 1/115th's outposts, isolated the battalion headquarters by cutting telephone lines, and broke into A Company's positions. A wild mêlée broke out, and part of the heavy mortar company attached to 1/115th made off to the north. At about 0200 hours, however, radio contact was established with 110th Artillery Battalion, and Johns called down fire onto his own positions. Faced with a combination of determined resistance, counter-attacks and American firepower, at 0430 hours the raiders withdrew, leaving behind 54 dead. 1/115th had lost 142 men.

1/115th was badly disrupted by the raid, and instead of attacking at 0600 hours, as planned, did not advance until noon. B Company led, followed by C, D and the remnants of A, all heading towards Belle Fontaine. The first hedge beyond the line of departure was unoccupied, but then opposition stiffened. One platoon was caught by a mortar concentration in a sunken lane and wiped out. 1/115th was dispirited by these events, and lost momentum. After gaining a few hedgerows the battalion stopped. Lt Col Arthur Sheppe's 3/115th moved up on the right of 1/115th, but was unable to capture la Luzerne. West of the D6, Major Maurice Clift's 2/115th advanced at 2000 hours, watched by German observers on Hill 122.

In the dense patch of orchards north of le Bourg d'Enfer the battalion came under fire from three sides, and fell back. Nowhere along 115th Regiment's front had the Americans managed to advance more than a few hundred metres.

American infantry moving up in open double file along a lane thickly screened by hedges, 11 July. The soldier on the left carries the barrel assembly of an M1917A1 .30-calibre machine gun, one of the standard support weapons used by US infantry units during the war. (USNA)

Things went better in 116th Regiment's sector. As Tour D (*pp. 166–84*) describes in further detail, after a 25-minute bombardment 2/116th advanced at 0600 hours against St-André-de-l'Épine, assisted by 743rd Tank Battalion. The battalion's main axis ran along the boundary between II/ and III/9th Paratroop Regiment, a vulnerable point in the German line. However, it took the attackers five hours to advance 500 metres, clearing the hedges as they went. By 1100 hours German resistance was weakening, and 2/116th pressed on to the crest of the ridge before turning west along the D195 towards Martinville. 1/116th and 3/116th also pushed on, then wheeled right. 1/116th followed 2nd Battalion while 3/116th headed further south, aiming for la Boulaye on the D972. However, 3/116th soon ran into stiff opposition. Although Gerhardt was optimistic, ordering his troops at 1920 hours to 'push on; if possible take St-Lô', by nightfall the exhausted Americans had stopped 1.5 km east of Martinville. 116th Infantry had gained almost 3 km but in doing so had opened up a gap to the east between it and 2nd Infantry Division on Hill 192. In the evening 2/175th Infantry Regiment went forward to cover this flank, digging in south of St-André-de-l'Épine. 1/175th and 3/175th were also placed on alert and told to be ready to attack south-west the next day.

By the end of 11 July, 29th Division had made a significant penetration of 3rd Paratroop Division's defences. However, further westward movement would only be possible if Hill 192 was secured. Fortunately, thanks to a superbly orchestrated attack by 2nd Infantry Division, this is precisely what was achieved on 11 July.

An M29 'Weasel' tracked cargo carrier escorts prisoners near St-Jean-de-Daye on 11 July. (USNA)

THE ATTACK ON HILL 192

Following the disappointment of 16 June, when 2nd Infantry Division was stopped on the slopes of Hill 192, there was relatively little fighting on US V Corps' front for several weeks. Late in the month, a minor redeployment of American units took place north of Hill 192, leaving 1/38th and 3/38th Infantry Regiment facing part of 9th Paratroop Regiment on the hill itself. Further east, 23rd Infantry Regiment was opposed at St-Georges-d'Elle and Bérigny by 5th Paratroop Regiment, while 9th Infantry Regiment and 8th Paratroop Regiment faced one another west of the River Drôme. East of the Drôme, responsibility for the German defence shifted from Seventh Army to Panzer Group West. Its 2nd Panzer Division manned the line against 1st Infantry Division at Caumont. On 1 July First US Army extended its front slightly to the east, allowing British 7th Armoured Division to go into reserve against an anticipated counter-blow. However, owing to the diversion of II SS Panzer Corps to halt the British 'Epsom' offensive, no counter-attack took place. Consequently, apart from patrol activity and a surprise assault on 1 July which gained 38th Infantry Regiment a few hundred metres north-west of Hill 192, this part of the battlefront remained fairly quiet.

This did not mean, however, that the Americans were doing nothing. Indeed, in accordance with Bradley's First Army plan and a V Corps' Field Order of 4 July, Maj Gen Robertson's 2nd Infantry Division headquarters worked hard to prepare another attack to capture Hill 192. On 6 July 2nd Infantry Division issued its own field order, followed almost immediately by detailed written orders from the units involved. Numerous briefings and conferences also took place, often down to squad level. On 7 July there was a meeting between representatives of 2nd and 29th Infantry Divisions, to co-ordinate plans. Meanwhile, 2nd Infantry Division trained hard for its return to battle.

2nd Infantry Division's attack was prepared in meticulous detail. Hill 192 was considered to be of decisive importance because it dominated approaches to St-Lô from north and east. The convex upper slopes gave excellent lines of sight, and American troops felt that the Germans always had them under close observation. The 16 June attack had failed, but had given Robertson's staff information about the terrain and German defensive tactics. Patrols also gained some intelligence, although the paratroopers opposed them with vigour. Air reconnaissance sorties on 22 and 25 June, and again on 7 July, provided most information. Many photographs were studied, positions spotted, and plotted onto 1:5000-scale maps. Company and platoon commanders also flew over the ground in spotter aircraft to familiarise themselves with the terrain.

US replacements watch a demonstration of a German 'S' mine. Despite an efficient replacement system, American infantry battalions sometimes fought at barely 50 per cent of their authorised strength, especially during the final stages of the battle for St-Lô. *(USNA)*

The terrain favoured defence. Hill 192 rises gently from 140 metres to 192 metres over 1 km, but the last slope up to the crest is steep. A diamond-shaped wood, 900 metres by 500 metres, the Bois du Soulaire, or 'Ford Woods' to 2nd Infantry Division, crowned the hill. A smaller wood, 'Dodge Woods', 150 metres to the west, gave cover to an artillery observation tower. Elsewhere the country was typical *bocage*, of the kind that had already caused the US troops so many problems. Two re-entrants – or draws to the Americans – cut the hill: one running broadly north–south through Cloville, known as 'Dead Man's Gulch' because of the heavy losses sustained here by 2/38th Infantry on 16 June; the other west–east across the D195, an obstacle to vehicles called 'Purple Heart Draw'. Despite intermittent rain, both draws were dry in July 1944.

The hill was defended by III/9th Paratroop Regiment, with I/5th Paratroop Regiment east of the D195. Each battalion had about 500 front-line troops, organised in three rifle companies plus a heavy weapons company. The rifle companies had many MG 42s, sub-machine guns and 50-mm mortars. According to US sources, the weapons company served two light howitzers, four 81-mm mortars and eight machine guns. Captured correspondence showed that the paratroops were confident, with high morale, and had worked hard to prepare their defences. Dugouts were typically four metres underground, with massive overhead cover. Firing positions were tunnelled into the corners of hedges, and were very well concealed. The firing slits could not be spotted, even with binoculars, from as close as one hedgerow away.

A screen of outposts, manned only by day, protected the main defences from reconnaissance patrols. Behind the screen was a network of strongpoints, built for all-round defence. One dominated Dead Man's Gulch from ground near le Parc farm; US troops called this 'Kraut Corner'. Another, the 'Four Fields Strongpoint', was north of Ford Woods. A third was south and east of Purple Heart Draw. Several buildings on the southern outskirts of St-Georges-d'Elle were fortified, with approaches blocked by wire and mines. The hamlets of le Soulaire, le Calvaire and Cloville, with their stoutly-constructed stone houses, were also prepared for defence. The sunken roads obstructed or channelled movement by vehicles, and provided firing points for mortars. Sections of the road from Cloville to St-Georges-d'Elle were enfiladed by 20-mm anti-aircraft cannon. The Germans had also registered the positions of numerous lanes and other features, allowing them to call down accurate mortar and artillery fire, some of it from batteries positioned south of the D972. A railway gun near Torigni-sur-Vire occasionally shelled the rear areas of V Corps.

Although 3rd Paratroop Division was confident and resolute, and Hill 192 was a strong position, there was a switch line of reserve positions in the hedgerows south of the D972. Not many of the men on the hill survived to make use of them.

The plan for Operation 'Nelson' was to attack on a fine day so as to make best use of air and artillery support. Ninth Air Force was to provide armed reconnaissance to survey and interdict roads south of the D972. Between H+15 and H+90 minutes four groups, each of 48 P-47 Thunderbolts, were to attack along a corridor 800 metres wide astride that road, using 250-kg bombs and white phosphorus. 2nd Infantry Division was to mark targets, spotted by air observation posts, with red smoke. Guns from V Corps and the divisional artillery were to fire a complex and intense programme in support of the infantry, while 1st Infantry and 2nd Armored Divisions conducted diversionary shoots to the east. V Corps' artillery, in total seven battalions of 155-mm guns, one of 8-inch howitzers and one of 4.5-inch guns, was engaged on counter-battery missions and long-range harassing fire for days in advance. For the last 20 minutes before H-Hour, all guns fired at maximum rate on the German forward positions, then the rolling barrage began. Ten battalions of 105-mm and 155-mm howitzers were available, with seven firing in direct support of the assault troops. The fire programme was perfected by Brig Gen George Hays, 2nd Infantry Division's artillery commander, and his staff.

Principal US Artillery Roles at Hill 192
11 July 1944

V Corps artillery
17th Field Artillery Observation Battalion

190th Field Artillery Group

190th FA Btn (155-mm)	*counter-battery and long-range fires*
200th FA Btn (155-mm)	*counter-battery and long-range fires*
997th FA Btn (8-inch)	*counter-mortar battery and long-range fires*

406th Field Artillery Group

941st FA Btn (4.5-inch)	*targets south of D972 + 9th Inf Regt sector*
186th FA Btn (155-mm)	*supporting 1st Inf Div*
955th FA Btn (155-mm)	*targets south of D972 + 9th Inf Regt sector*
987th FA Btn (155-mm)	*supporting 2nd Armd Div*

187th Field Artillery Group

187th FA Btn (155-mm)	*direct support of 2nd Inf Div*
953rd FA Btn (155-mm)	*direct support of 2nd Inf Div; see also below*

Other artillery
From Corps artillery

953rd FA Btn (155-mm)	*general support and reinforcing 38th FA Bn*

2nd Infantry Division artillery

12th FA Btn (155-mm)	*general support and reinforcing 38th FA Bn*
15th FA Btn (105-mm)	*direct support of 9th Inf Regt and reinforce 37th FA Bn*
37th FA Btn (105-mm)	*direct support of 23rd Inf Regt*
38th FA Btn (105-mm)	*direct support of 38th Inf Regt*

1st Infantry Division artillery

5th FA Btn (155-mm)	*reinforce 15th FA Bn on 9th Inf Regt front*
7th FA Btn (105-mm)	*reinforce 15th FA Bn on 9th Inf Regt front*
62nd FA Btn (105-mm)	*direct support 38th FA Bn*

3rd Armored Division artillery

54th FA Btn (105-mm)	*reinforce 38th FA Bn*
67th FA Btn (105-mm)	*reinforce 38th FA Bn*

One of his officers later described it as 'a [First] World War rolling barrage with modern instincts.' These 'instincts' were new means of controlling and adjusting fire:

'First, the 1:5000 maps of the area were marked with east–west lines 100 yards apart from the line of departure to the objective; these lines were lettered. The light [105-mm] battalions were each designated a colour [representing a zone of fire] and an area, which was delimited by north–south lines. Thus, if any infantry unit was held up, or advanced faster than anticipated, a simple scheme was provided for holding or lifting the barrage.'

Source: 2nd Infantry Division combat interviews, RG 407, Box 24014, Folder 12, USNA.

To control the barrage, the infantry were trained to call up fire, and observers with the companies could speak directly to the batteries supporting them, rather than requesting fire missions through a centralised fire direction centre as was the usual American system. This meant the guns were quicker to respond. The scale of the artillery support was unprecedented; over 25,000 shells were fired during the attack.

The actual assault on Hill 192 would be carried out by 38th Infantry Regiment in the west, with two battalions forward, flanked to the east by a battalion of 23rd Infantry Regiment. As discussed earlier in this chapter, 29th Infantry Division attacked simultaneously on 38th Regiment's right. 2nd Infantry Division's assault troops were supported by 741st Tank Battalion, 2nd Engineer Combat Battalion and the 4.2-inch mortars of 81st Chemical Battalion. 612th Tank Destroyer Battalion provided protection against mechanised counter-attack. East of 23rd Infantry's sector, 9th Infantry Regiment would demonstrate against the Germans and give fire support as requested.

The assault was to use new and carefully rehearsed tactics, derived from study of the recent fighting. Analysing the events of 16 June, 2nd Infantry Division staff concluded: 'The initial assaults were unimaginative and we suffered simply because we had no ready-made solution to the hedgerow.' By early July new tactics had been devised, based on all-arms teams at low level. On 28 June, 2nd Infantry Division began intensive training in the new fighting methods, which used groups consisting of one tank, an infantry squad and four engineers.

HISTORY

The new attack drill was:

'Engineers would blow the hedges for the tanks to pass through, the tanks would fire their 75-mm guns into hedgerow corners and spray the next hedgerow to cover the infantry advance, and the infantry would protect the tanks from bazooka men and then close with the enemy.'

Source: 2nd Infantry Division combat interviews, RG 407, Box 24104, Folder 12, USNA.

Conical prongs welded to the front of each tank made holes suitable for the placement of demolition charges in the hedge banks, and each Sherman carried enough amatol on its hull to blow nine such gaps. Infantry scouted forward along the sides of fields, covered by BARs and the tank machine guns. Once the forward hedge was clear, three of the engineers advanced, found a suitable place for gapping, and then called the tank forward, usually by waving a handkerchief to the fourth engineer, who remained with the vehicle. He communicated with the tank crew using a telephone attached to the rear of the engine deck. Although the terrain and tactics made it inevitable that 'the assault boiled down to a series of squad battles all along', it was important to co-ordinate these actions. If the squads did not keep alignment, they would be vulnerable to counter-attacks on their flank and rear. The new tactics worked in training, and bonded the riflemen, tankers and engineers into confident units, which were kept together for use in battle.

38th Infantry Regiment had primary responsibility for capturing Hill 192. Two battalions were involved, with 2/38th attacking in the west at H-Hour (0630) and 1/38th to the east at H+20 minutes (in the event, the actual timings differed). Support was tailored to the circumstances; 2/38th had more tanks and engineers attached, and priority in calling for assistance from the cannon and anti-tank companies and dedicated artillery. 3/38th, plus some light tanks, was to follow to mop up stragglers, stop counter-attacks from the south and west, and then occupy the crest once the forward units were on their objectives on the D972. The assault battalions each deployed with two companies up, on a front of 365 metres; reserve companies followed a few hundred metres behind. 1/38th intended to advance in squad columns and deploy fully when south of Dodge Woods. 2/38th would move directly to the D972, dig in and prepare to defend. The companies would deploy two platoons forward and one back, the platoons with two squads up and one behind. Each assault company had three tanks allocated, others being held in reserve. Engineers would clear mines, improve roads, help vehicles get forward, and strengthen field-works on the objectives. Anti-tank detachments were on hand to protect the infantry, and then guard the roads leading south from the D972.

23rd Infantry Regiment's field order was equally specific. The main attack was to be carried out by 1st Battalion, advancing south to the D972. 3/23rd was to follow, clearing any remaining pockets of resistance and guarding the east flank. If 1/23rd was held up and 1/38th was getting ahead, 3/23rd was to manoeuvre to lead the assault. The 3rd Battalion was also to carry out a diversionary attack in the eastern part of St-Georges-d'Elle, with heavy machine-gun support. The cannon company would shell Purple Heart Draw from H-20 minutes to H-5, as would the attached mortar company. 1/23rd planned to advance with C and A Companies forward, accompanied by tanks and engineers.

Medics administer blood plasma to a wounded GI, while another looks on (photo taken 11 July). *(USNA)*

Intermittent rain forced two postponements of the operation but, despite an uninspiring forecast, on 10 July US troops were told there would be no further delay. Thus, in what one source described as a 'wet San Francisco fog', at 0400 hours on 11 July the assault

HISTORY

battalions began moving into their assembly areas. Soon after, the guns opened up, pulverising the German defences and raising American morale. Owing to low cloud and poor visibility, all air-directed shoots were cancelled. The P-47 close air support missions were also postponed. Later, aircraft were called up to attack a marked target on the D972, but bombed short, hitting 2/38th's command post and 1/38th's aid station. Consequently, the rest of the P-47 operations were cancelled.

The view south from the positions held by 2/38th Infantry at the end of 11 July, with the church of St-Jean-des-Baisants in the distance. The Germans used the high ground south of the D972 to observe and shell US troops advancing along the Martinville Ridge during the final phase of the battle for St-Lô. (ST)

At 0600 hours 2nd Infantry Division's attack began. As detailed in Tour C (pp. 150–66), the assault was a great success. Although the German strongpoints resisted strongly, elsewhere opposition crumbled, allowing the resistance nests to be outflanked. On the right, 2/38th ran into trouble at Kraut Corner soon after the attack began, but overran the position in fierce fighting and pushed on through Cloville. 1/38th lost some of its tank support to German fire, but continued behind the rolling barrage towards Ford Woods. By midday the new assault tactics and devastating artillery support had resulted in a breakthrough, with American troops on top of Hill 192 and advancing towards the D972. At 1700 hours the first troops of 2/38th Infantry reached the road, where they were joined by the rest of the battalion and some tanks. Although 1/38th did not advance quite so far, by nightfall it had dug in south of Ford Woods, only 200 metres from the road. On the left flank, 1/23rd

Infantry also made good ground against tough opposition, and got past Purple Heart Draw. Only on the extreme left, where 3/23rd lacked significant artillery support, was progress especially painful. Here, in an indication of what might otherwise have happened to the main assault force, one platoon of I Company suffered 32 casualties, compared with only 51 in the entire 1st Battalion. L/23rd also lost 23 men during its limited attack at St-Georges-d'Elle, but sucessfully prevented elements of I/5th Paratroop Regiment from disengaging and assisting their comrades to the west.

It is sometimes suggested that there are 'no atheists in foxholes'. Here, a soldier of 2nd Infantry Division's 38th Regiment reads his prayer book after the successful attack on Hill 192. *(USNA)*

II Paratroop Corps had initially faced 2nd Infantry Division's assault with confidence, reporting at 1200 hours that its local reserves were well placed to launch a counter-attack. However, the Germans could do little when confronted with the raw power of the American offensive. 3rd Paratroop Division's artillery was relatively weak and the intensity of US artillery and mortar fire on its defences and rear areas was unprecedented. Reinforcements were sent forward, and consumed in the battle. During the day the troops in place were reinforced by elements of 12th Paratroop Assault Gun Brigade, 3rd Paratroop Engineer Battalion and 3rd Paratroop Reconnaissance Company, all to no avail. One company of 5th Paratroop Regiment, for example, was reduced from 170 men to 30.

Faced with the simultaneous penetration by US 29th Division nearer St-Lô, 3rd Paratroop Division fell back to a new line from Bérigny to la Boulaye on the D972. Rommel had ordered Seventh Army to defend the hill at all costs, but it could not be done. At 1900 hours *General* Meindl reported to Seventh Army that he deemed it 'impossible to hold the present line tomorrow, should the enemy apply additional material.' *SS-Oberstgruppenführer* Hausser, however, was confronted with worse problems elsewhere, and informed Army Group B that 'no extraordinary measures seem necessary at II Paratroop Corps'. Possibly aware of this apparent lack of concern, Meindl telephoned again at midnight, stating that 'The situation is becoming increasingly poor... Our losses of personnel, weapons and material are enormous.' He also asked for the transfer of 14th Paratroop Regiment (5th Paratroop Division) to reinforce his front. Hausser remained unimpressed. As Seventh Army's telephone log bluntly records, 'Army refused to grant this request. There are no other forces available.'

For 2nd US Infantry Division, Operation Nelson was costly in ammunition but not in casualties. Its 23rd and 38th Regiments lost 304 men (including 61 killed; figures for supporting units are unavailable), but the capture of Hill 192 cleared the eastern flank for 29th Infantry Division's assault along the Martinville Ridge, the indirect approach to St-Lô. Not without reason did Maj Gen Robertson later describe the attack as 'The most methodically planned and professionally executed job the division has ever done.'

Overall, 11 July was a day of calamity for Seventh Army, and great success for the Americans. First Army had been delayed west of the Vire, and disappointed in the sectors of 35th Infantry Division and 115th Infantry Regiment, but had won Hill 192 and half the Martinville Ridge. Seventh Army had made its strongest mobile counter-attack, and failed miserably. There were no reserves available on the German side, and few reinforcements on the way. The Americans were closing in on St-Lô. The best Seventh Army could do was to delay the loss of the town.

CHAPTER 6

THE LAST PHASE, 12–18 JULY

By 12 July First US Army's offensive was winding down. Although it had failed to achieve Lt Gen Bradley's aim of a breakthrough into Brittany, significant progress had been made through the *bocage*, and considerable damage done to Seventh Army's fighting power. On the night of 13–14 July LXXXIV Corps' left wing withdrew behind the Ay and the Sèves Rivers near the west coast of the Cotentin, allowing US VIII Corps to get within 2 km of the D900 Lessay–St-Lô highway, designated by Bradley as the start line for his next attack. Maj Gen Collins' VII Corps also continued its advance, pushing along the road from Carentan to Périers, which also lay on the D900. With planning well under way for Operation Cobra, on 15 July First Army's offensive halted west of the River Taute, and US troops settled down for a brief period of well-deserved rest.

Members of 3rd Armored Division's reconnaissance battalion display a sign telling the Germans that they are surrounded and should surrender (photo taken 14 July). *(USNA)*

East of the Taute, however, intense fighting continued from 12–18 July. Here, the soldiers of VII and XIX Corps battled hard to reach the D900 and to capture St-Lô. Several organisational changes took place during this period, the most significant being the transfer of 30th Infantry Division from XIX to VII Corps late on 15 July. Thereafter, all attacks west of the Vire took place under the direction of Maj Gen Collins' staff. East of the Vire the main development was on 14 July, when 35th Infantry Division's 134th Infantry Regiment entered the line from corps reserve. It took over the assault on Hill 122, allowing 29th Infantry Division to concentrate on the battle east of the D6. On the opposite side of the line, the Germans also altered their dispositions in an attempt to maintain their defences. On 15–16 July 352nd Division gave up 1.5 km of front to 3rd Paratroop Division, and withdrew its main line of resistance between the D6 and the N174 by 1 km. Despite such measures, however, Seventh Army could not stop the American

From 9 July onwards, 9th Infantry Division fought hard to clear the east bank of the River Taute and to push south on 30th Infantry Division's right flank. Bitter resistance from 17th SS Panzergrenadier Division and Panzer Lehr slowed its attack, and the Americans only made significant progress from 17 July. Here, 105-mm field howitzers of 84th Field Artillery Battalion support 9th Infantry Division's advance on 13 July. (USNA)

advance. By the end of 17 July US troops were close to the D900 west of the Vire, and 352nd Division had lost Hill 122. The next day, 29th Division thrust into St-Lô, and within 24 hours the town was firmly in its hands. Although neither side knew it at the time, this marked the end of the positional-attritional phase of the Battle of Normandy, and the start of the Allied break-out.

GRINDING DOWN THE OPPOSITION, 12–14 JULY

On 12 July 2nd Infantry Division consolidated its hold on Hill 192. The Germans knew they could not defend the salient between Bérigny and St-Georges-d'Elle, and wanted to release troops to shore up their crumbling positions further west. Consequently, when Maj Gen Robertson's troops advanced again at 1100 hours they met little opposition. By nightfall, 38th Infantry Regiment was established along the D972 between le Calvaire and the Bois du Soulaire, while 23rd Infantry Regiment occupied the highway from la Croix Rouge to the outskirts of Bérigny. Here, to II Paratroop Corps' relief, V Corps stopped its advance, satisfied that it had secured the left flank of XIX Corps' offensive to the west.

Despite 2nd Infantry Division's achievement, however, when 29th Infantry Division resumed its attack towards St-Lô on 12 July, it made disappointing progress. As described in detail in Tour D, although 116th Infantry Regiment's assault along the Martinville Ridge had the virtue of outflanking the defences at Hill 122, it also exposed the US troops to artillery and mortar fire from the high ground further south, near la Barre-de-Semilly. Combined with fierce resistance from 3rd Paratroop Engineer Battalion, this stopped the Americans within 500 metres of their overnight positions. Two battalions of 175th Infantry Regiment came up in support, and on 13 July launched their own drive west along the D972. But bad weather caused the anticipated air support to be cancelled, and the attack stalled. Meanwhile, after occupying la Luzerne and Belle Fontaine, 1/ and 3/115th Infantry's attempts to push further south met intense fire from German troops at Martinville, and were suspended. West of the D6, 2/115th also suffered a series of setbacks. On 12 July the battalion pushed through le Bourg d'Enfer onto Hill 122, but was heavily counter-attacked and thrown back to its original positions. After re-organising, it tried again next day, supported by the rest of the regiment astride the D6. Bitter resistance from Battlegroup *Böhm*, however, halted the Americans after a few hedgerows. In the evening Major Clift, commander of 2/115th Infantry, and his executive officer were both replaced – yet more victims, it seemed, of Maj Gen Gerhardt's intolerance of alleged 'under-performance' in the battle for St-Lô.

While 29th Division struggled to maintain the momentum of 11 July, similar difficulties were encountered by US forces further west. This was especially true west of the Vire, where 30th Infantry Division attempted to extend its foothold on the ridge leading south from les Hauts Vents. Owing to the limited space between the Terrette and Vire rivers, which channelled the advance along a predictable route only 2 km wide, progress on 12–13 July was slow. The Germans were relatively strong in this area, Panzer Lehr having remained at the front after its failed attack on the 11th. They also controlled the country west of the Terrette and east of the Vire, and poured fire into the flanks of 30th Division as it attacked; 18 battalions of guns firing counter-battery missions could not silence them. Despite determined efforts, by the evening of 13 July 119th Infantry Regiment still had not cleared Pont-Hébert or captured the bridge across the Vire. Further west, 117th Infantry was also unable to gain control over the Terrette valley. After being

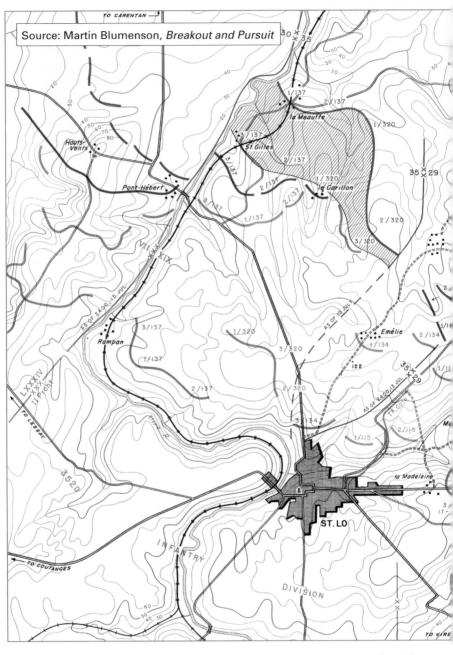

Source: Martin Blumenson, *Breakout and Pursuit*

counter-attacked, Maj Gen Hobbs decided that his forces should dig in and give 9th Infantry Division, advancing from le Dézert on the west of the Terrette, a chance to come abreast. Consequently, apart from at Pont-Hébert, where fighting continued, on 14 July 30th Infantry Division rested and re-organised, prior to resuming its offensive the next day.

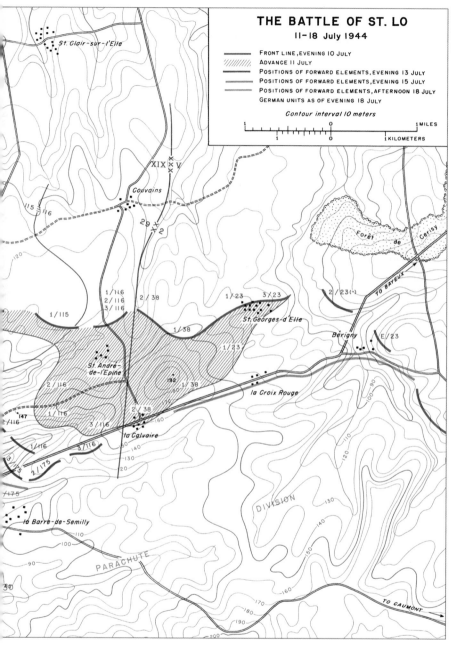

THE BATTLE OF ST. LO
11–18 July 1944

FRONT LINE, EVENING 10 JULY
ADVANCE 11 JULY
POSITIONS OF FORWARD ELEMENTS, EVENING 13 JULY
POSITIONS OF FORWARD ELEMENTS, EVENING 15 JULY
POSITIONS OF FORWARD ELEMENTS, AFTERNOON 18 JULY
GERMAN UNITS AS OF EVENING 18 JULY

Contour interval 10 meters

1 MILES
1 KILOMETERS

St. Clair-sur-l'Elle

XIX V

Couvains

29 2

Forêt de Cerisy

115 116

120

1/116
2/116
3/116

2/38

1/23   3/23

2/23(-)

TO BAYEUX

1/115

1/38

St. Georges-d'Elle

Bérigny

E/23

1/23

St. André-de-l'Epine

192

1/38

2/116

la Croix Rouge

147

1/116

2/116

3/116

2/38

la Calvaire

1/116

3/116

2/175

175

to Barre-de-Semilly

DIVISION

PARACHUTE

TO CAUMONT

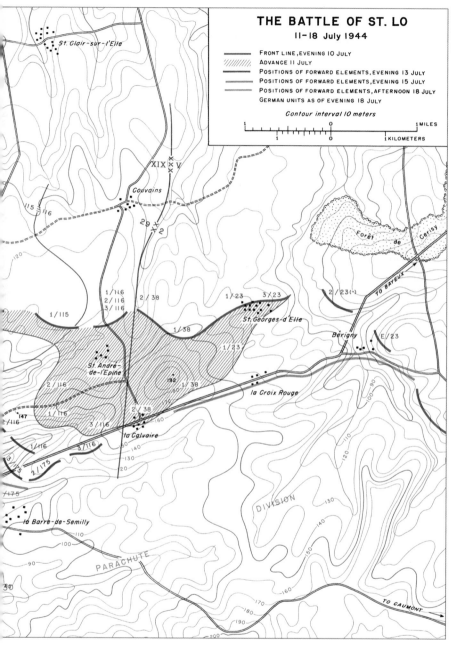

Due north of St-Lô, however, 35th Infantry Division enjoyed rather greater success during this period. Although 1/320th and 2/137th Infantry were unable to capture the le Carillon strongpoint, they drove back German outposts and gained some ground. More important, after a heavy artillery bombardment early on 12 July, 1/137th secured St-Gilles, while 3/137th pushed forward on its left.

The next day the Americans struck again, but made little progress. On 14 July, however, when 137th Infantry attacked for a third time, 352nd Infantry Division's front buckled. Assisted by B/737th Tank Battalion, 1/ and 3/137th Infantry achieved significant gains. Seventh Army's war diary recorded the loss of Point 51, overlooking the Vire near Pont-Hébert, at 2200 hours, and by midnight the Americans held a 1-km stretch of the N174 east of the river. Simultaneously, elements of 119th Infantry finally overcame resistance at the western end of the bridge at Pont-Hébert, leaving the crossing firmly in US hands.

An infantry orders group studies air photographs before an attack, 15 July. The officer second from left (Lt Col Edward Gill, 175th Infantry) carries a 'K-Bar' combat knife next to his pistol, while the man with his back to the camera has a walkie-talkie radio slung over his shoulder. *(USNA)*

These successes were less dramatic than those of 11 July, but nevertheless seriously damaged the Germans' ability to defend St-Lô. US casualties were severe, but so were their enemy's – and unlike the Americans, the Germans could expect little reinforcement. According to Seventh Army's war diary, by 13 July 3rd Paratroop Division had suffered 4,064 casualties, with even heavier losses among 352nd Infantry Division and its attached battlegroups. Replacements were few, and while it welcomed the arrival of 5th Paratroop Division, Seventh Army was worried that it was seriously under-trained. Furthermore, the loss of the Pont-Hébert bridge and the US advance to the N174 were particularly disconcerting developments for II Paratroop Corps. Not only did they threaten to outflank le Carillon, but they also compromised 352nd Infantry Division's position in the Vire bend. German engineers had constructed an underwater bridge to facilitate movement across the river at Rampan, 2.5 km south of Pont-Hebert, but its capacity was limited. Consequently, any further advance towards St-Lô west of the Vire carried the risk that the Germans in this area would be encircled, with no way of extracting their heavy equipment. In the face of this threat, *General* Meindl decided to pull his forces back to a line closer to that held by LXXXIV Corps west of the Vire, and as well as ordering the evacuation of le Carillon, he instructed a 1-km withdrawal by 352nd Infantry Division the next day. However, he also decided that it was now more important than ever to hold Hill 122, which dominated the approaches to St-Lô from the north, while LXXXIV Corps tried to stabilise the situation further west. On 14 July he therefore deployed the remnants of 30th Mobile Brigade, newly returned from west of the Vire, to Hill 122, along with some additional artillery. Here they joined 916th Grenadiers in a last-ditch attempt to preserve a front against XIX Corps' attacks from the north.

View south-west across the Vire from Rampan churchyard. On 17 July, 30th Infantry Division captured the underwater bridge here, prompting a retirement by 352nd Infantry Division to the final defence line north of St-Lô. *(Author)*

On the American side, the events of 12–14 July convinced Maj Gen Corlett that, although continued efforts should be made to capture St-Lô from the east, and to extend the advance in 30th

HISTORY

Division's sector, it was also necessary to capture Hill 122. On 14 July, while the exhausted soldiers of 29th Division enjoyed a rest day, Colonel Butler Miltonberger's 134th Infantry therefore entered the line near Villiers-Fossard. Here it relieved the overstretched and depleted battalions of 115th Infantry, allowing these to redeploy on a narrow front east of the D6, which became the new divisional boundary. The 134th was reinforced by most of 737th Tank Battalion, plus elements of 654th Tank Destroyer Battalion and the 4.2-inch mortars of 92nd Chemical Battalion; the force was known collectively as Task Force Sebree, after the assistant divisional commander, Brig Gen Edmund Sebree. According to Maj Gen Baade's Field Order No. 4, 134th Infantry was to attack Hill 122 on 15 July. Meanwhile, Maj Gen Gerhardt's forces would renew their thrust along the Martinville Ridge, while 30th Division continued its attempts to reach the D900 west of the Vire.

Sergeant E. Vandenberg uses an abandoned German foxhole in St-Lô's town cemetery for protection against artillery fire and sniper activity, 23 July. *(USNA)*

THE FALL OF ST-LÔ, 15–18 JULY

US XIX Corps' offensive resumed at 0515 hours on 15 July, preceded by a short but furious artillery bombardment. On the right, 30th Infantry Division battered its way forward against elements of Panzer Lehr, which was supported by III/14th Paratroop Regiment. The Germans fought strongly until midday, but gave way in the afternoon. 117th Infantry Regiment reached the outskirts of le Mesnil-Durand and captured la Hucherie, then dug in while 120th Infantry came forward to take up the attack the next day. LXXXIV Corps was now near breaking point. At 2330 hours, GenLt von Choltitz told *Generalmajor* Max Pemsel, Seventh Army's chief of staff, that 'there is nobody left. In the event that no further resources are made available, the unit will be annihilated because it will not retreat. The entire battle is a terrific bloodbath.' Responding to this warning, Seventh Army released another battalion of 5th Paratroop Division from reserve. However, its war diary showed little evidence of optimism, observing that such reinforcements were quickly used up, and that few additional reserves remained. Not for the first time, it also bemoaned the continued failure of the *Luftwaffe*, which remained as conspicuous by its absence as it had been throughout the battle for St-Lô.

A frightened-looking German youngster surrenders on the north-eastern outskirts of St-Lô, 18 July. *(USNA)*

In 29th Infantry Division's sector there was also some evidence that, for all their resilience and skill, the Germans were close to collapse. Although 3rd Paratroop Division deployed reinforcements from quieter sectors of the front, it was unable to hold all its positions against determined US attacks. As described in Tour D, during the evening of 15 July elements of 2/116th Infantry penetrated the German defences on the Martinville Ridge and established themselves on the D972. Schimpf's men closed the gap, but were too weak to destroy the 200 or so lightly armed Americans, and consoled themselves with the fact that they had isolated the breakthrough. Further north, 115th Infantry also made some progress on the 15th, advancing about 500 metres and taking a considerable number of prisoners. However, Maj Gen Gerhardt was disappointed that his men had not achieved more and, when the Germans counter-attacked on the Martinville Ridge the next day, it seemed they were far from beaten. Nevertheless, all these counter-attacks failed, and Gerhardt was convinced that one more push would see his division in St-Lô. Despite the fact that most of his infantry battalions were 50 per cent under-strength, late on 16 July he called for a maximum effort the following morning. Simultaneously, he ordered the formation of a mobile reserve. Taking its name from the division's assistant commander, Task Force Cota (or Task Force C) comprised elements of 29th Cavalry Reconnaissance Troop and 121st Engineer Battalion, a few artillery observers and military policemen, and platoons from the 175th Infantry's Cannon and Anti-Tank Companies. Attached units, including some Shermans from 747th Tank Battalion, B/803rd Tank Destroyer Battalion and the Reconnaissance Platoon of 821st Tank Destroyer Battalion, provided heavy firepower. Assembling near Couvains, Task Force Cota's role was to exploit any breakthrough achieved by the infantry regiments on 17 July.

Though it is less than clear, one motivating factor behind Gerhardt's decision to maintain his offensive may well have been the success achieved by the recently-arrived 35th Infantry Division on 15–16 July. Launching their attack on a two-regiment front, Baade's men had mixed fortunes on the 15th. In the west, despite 352nd Infantry Division's withdrawal, all attempts by 137th Infantry to push into the Vire bend failed in the face of heavy fire directed from Hill 122. However, when 134th Infantry began its own assault, it made rapid progress. Punching south-west behind a rolling barrage, 1/134th and its accompanying armour advanced

An M10 tank destroyer attached to Task Force Cota fighting into St-Lô. Note the empty shell cases from the M10's 3-inch gun. *(USNA)*

along the track (now the D191) running from Villiers-Fossard towards St-Lô. At 1250 hours its commander, Lt Col Boatsman, reported that the battalion was through the hamlet of Émilié and only 550 metres from the top of Hill 122. Corlett and Baade were delighted, and ordered Colonel Miltonberger to send 3/134th forward from reserve. Urged on by Brig Gen Sebree, at 2100 hours 1/134th renewed its assault, and by midnight was digging in just short of the hilltop. A few hours later the Germans counter-attacked, but the Americans held their positions, and followed up by pushing their outposts over the crest of the hill. On 16 July, 3/134th came forward, clearing heavy opposition behind 1/134th's front, and by mid-afternoon was consolidating near Émilié. Meanwhile, 2/134th advanced on the left, capturing les Romains and bridging the gap between 1/134th and 115th Infantry Regiment east of the D6.

The Germans fought desperately to halt 35th Infantry Division's attack, carrying out numerous small-scale counter-attacks and hammering the US positions with artillery fire. However, though they averted a complete collapse, it was obvious that the position in the Vire bend was becoming increasingly precarious. When 30th Infantry Division (now under VII Corps) renewed its assault on the

Tanks and infantry of Task Force Cota moving along the D6 reach the junction with the D972 in St-Lô, 18 July. *(USNA)*

16th, throwing back Panzer Lehr and its attached paratroops beyond le Mesnil-Durand and threatening the crossing at Rampan, II Paratroop Corps concluded that the previous day's withdrawal by 352nd Infantry Division might not be enough, and that unless Panzer Lehr's front was restored on 17 July, a further retreat to a line running along the south bank of the Vire to the northern outskirts of St-Lô should take place. However, when Army Group B was informed at 2350 hours on 16 July that Seventh Army was contemplating another retrograde movement, Rommel's HQ could offer no reassurance or support. Indeed, when GenMaj Pemsel stressed that a major US attack was expected on 18 July across the entire army front, Army Group B simply replied that the same thing was anticipated in Panzer Group West's sector. The implication, clearly, was that Seventh Army was on its own, and could expect little in the way of physical assistance in the next few days.

On 17 July the Americans attacked again. Early in the morning, 3/116th Infantry infiltrated through the German front near Martinville, joining 2/116th astride the D972 (*for details, see pp. 180–2*). 29th Division HQ was optimistic that the two battalions could continue into St-Lô. However, barely had the order to do so been given, than mortar and artillery rounds began falling among the Americans, killing 3/116th's commander, Major Thomas Howie, and compelling the US troops to switch to the defensive. Elements of 175th Infantry Regiment tried to move south-west along the D972 in support, but 3rd Paratroop Division stopped them, and in the afternoon carried out counter-attacks against the isolated US troops. These were driven off, partly by USAAF fighter-bombers summoned by radio, and by nightfall the positions held by 2/116th and 3/116th seemed relatively secure. Further north, however, the Germans repulsed most of the attacks by 115th Infantry Regiment, which continued to try to battle its way into St-Lô from the north-east. Only in the evening, when 2/115th carried out a bold left-flanking move that carried it to la Planche du Bois, barely a kilometre from St-Lô's eastern outskirts, did the US troops start to make significant progress. By then, however, any prospect of capturing the city that day had evaporated, so the Americans dug in, ready to make another push on 18 July.

For Seventh Army, however, the decision to pull back had already been taken. In part, this was an acknowledgement that 3rd Paratroop Division was simply too weak to hold Gerhardt's men any longer. However, events on 352nd Infantry Division's front and west of the Vire also had a significant impact. Here, US troops continued to make steady progress during 17 July against weakening opposition, notably in 30th Infantry Division's sector. When the Germans received reports that American troops (from 120th Infantry Regiment) had pushed south of Rampan, site of the under-water bridge, a crisis loomed. This was compounded when reports arrived that other bridges across the Vire south of St-Lô had been destroyed by US artillery fire, thus threatening the complete isolation of II Paratroop Corps from the rest of Seventh Army to the west. At 1000 hours, responding to a request from Seventh Army, Army Group B forbade the further withdrawal of 352nd Infantry Division. However, when a few hours later it became clear that the situation was irrecoverable, it changed its mind. In a conversation with Seventh Army's chief of staff at 1750 hours, *Oberst* Hans-Georg von Tempelhoff, Army Group B's Operations Officer, advised that there was no point in seeking permission from higher authorities, but that II Paratroop Corps should 'take whatever measures you think are necessary. If you have to withdraw, go ahead; just report to us afterwards that the enemy penetrated your Main Line of

Resistance [MLR] in several places and that you barely succeeded in re-establishing a new line to the rear.' Later, at 2100 hours, Field Marshal von Kluge – who had just taken direct control of Army Group B after Rommel was wounded earlier that day – attempted to intervene, ordering that the existing MLR must be held, and suggesting that reinforcements from Panzer Group West might soon be on their way. But by then it was too late; 352nd Infantry Division's exhausted units had already retreated to the northern outskirts of St-Lô or, in some cases, to positions south of the city. Grudgingly, von Kluge accepted the situation as a *fait accompli*.

A US infantryman advances past a dead German soldier at the church of St-Georges-Montcoq, probably on 18 July. *(USNA)*

The streets of St-Lô cleared of rubble for motor traffic. Without free movement of motor transport through the town it would have been very difficult for First US Army to sustain its advance after Operation Cobra began. *(USNA)*

As 352nd Infantry Division and 3rd Paratroop Division were attempting to create a close perimeter defence on the morning of 18 July, the Americans prepared to deliver a *coup de grâce*. While VII Corps thrust to the D900 west of the Vire and elements of 35th Infantry Division advanced without opposition into the Vire bend, 134th Infantry Regiment pushed down the slopes from Hill 122 into St-Georges-Montcoq. Meanwhile, 115th Infantry Regiment fought its way south-west astride the D6. By midday, Maj Gen Gerhardt was sure the city was about to fall, and ordered Task Force Cota to start moving. At 1510 hours the task force left Couvains, moved west and then dashed under harassing artillery fire down the D6 into St-Lô, collecting 1/115th *en route*. The task force was in the town by 1800 hours, and set up a base in the square near the cemetery, at the D6/D972 intersection. Men of 29th Cavalry Reconnaissance Troop went forward on foot and found several small German strongpoints. 1/115th, supported by tanks and tank destroyers, reduced these without too much difficulty, and occupied eighteen other key points, among them the still-intact bridges over the Vire. Artillery observers also went into one of the cathedral towers, from which they saw and engaged elements of 352nd Infantry Division assembling for a counter-attack on the south side of the city.

Remarkably, the Germans had not yet conceded St-Lô; at 1825 hours Meindl was asserting his determination to maintain an outpost line north of St-Lô, while Hausser insisted that 'the city is not to be given up as yet.' But 352nd Infantry Division lacked the strength and motivation to win it back, and hopes that it might meant that some of its remaining outposts to the north were cut off and lost. On 19 July, II Paratroop Corps shelled the town while patching together a line along the heights to the south. Maj Gen Gerhardt had already claimed his victory; on 18 July he signalled to Corlett: 'I have the honor to announce to the Corps Commander that Task Force "C" of the 29th Infantry Division has secured the city of St-Lô after 43 days of continual combat from the beaches to St-Lô. 29 Let's Go!' Finally, Bradley's forces had achieved their objectives. After six weeks of some of the bloodiest and most difficult fighting in the Battle of Normandy, the decisive battle for the liberation of France could now begin.

The body of Major Thomas D. Howie, commander of 3/116th Infantry when he was killed on 17 July, lies in state on the rubble of the church of St-Croix in St-Lô. He had promised to be the first man in his battalion to enter the town, and his body was carried into St-Lô on a jeep late on 18 July, on the direct instructions of Maj Gen Gerhardt. *(USNA)*

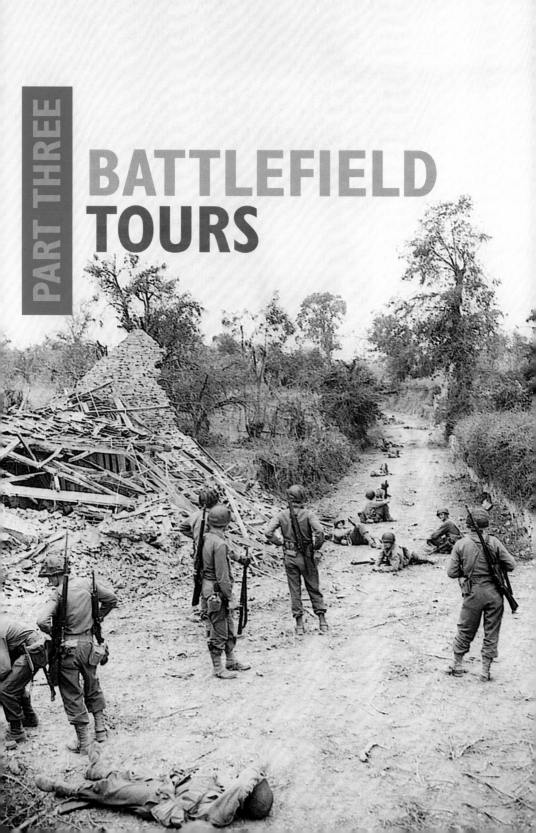

PART THREE

BATTLEFIELD TOURS

GENERAL TOURING INFORMATION

Normandy is a thriving holiday area, with some beautiful countryside, excellent beaches and very attractive architecture (particularly in the case of religious buildings). It was also, of course, the scene of heavy fighting in 1944, and this has had a considerable impact on the tourist industry. To make the most of your trip, especially if you intend visiting non-battlefield sites, we strongly recommend you purchase one of the general Normandy guidebooks that are commonly available. These include: *Michelin Green Guide: Normandy*; *Thomas Cook Travellers: Normandy*; *The Rough Guide to Brittany and Normandy*; *Lonely Planet: Normandy*.

TRAVEL REQUIREMENTS

First, make sure you have the proper documentation to enter France as a tourist. Citizens of European Union countries, including Great Britain, should not usually require visas, but will need to carry and show their passports. Others should check with the French Embassy in their own country before travelling. British citizens should also fill in and take Form E111 (available from main post offices), which deals with entitlement to medical treatment, and all should consider taking out comprehensive travel insurance. France is part of the Eurozone, and you should also check exchange rates before travelling.

GETTING THERE

The most direct routes from the UK to Lower Normandy are by ferry from Portsmouth to Ouistreham (near Caen), and from Portsmouth or Poole to Cherbourg. Depending on which you choose, and whether you travel by day or night, the crossing takes between four and seven hours. Alternatively, you can sail to Le Havre, Boulogne or Calais and drive the rest of the way. (Travel time from Calais to Caen is about four hours; motorway and bridge tolls may be payable depending on the exact route taken.) Another option is to use the Channel Tunnel. However you decide to travel, early booking is advised, especially during the summer months.

Although you can of course hire motor vehicles in Normandy, the majority of visitors from the UK or other EU countries will probably take their own. If you do so, you will also need to take: a full driving licence; your vehicle registration document; a certificate of motor insurance valid in France (your insurer will advise on this); spare headlight and indicator bulbs; headlight beam adjusters or tape; a warning triangle; and a sticker or number plate identifying which country the vehicle is registered in. Visitors from elsewhere should consult a motoring organisation in their home country for details of the documents and other items they will require.

Above: The abbey of St-Fromond was the scene of heavy fighting on 7-8 July. This splendid Norman church has fine restored wall paintings and is open on Tuesdays, Thursdays and Saturdays. *(Author)*

Page 113: US troops from 35th Infantry Division pause during the advance to St-Lô. The country is typical *bocage*, with sight lines of less than 100 metres. *(USNA)*

Normandy's road system is well developed, although there are still a few choke points, especially around the larger towns during rush hour and in the holiday season. As a general guide, in clear conditions it is possible to drive from Cherbourg to Caen in less than two hours.

ACCOMMODATION

Accommodation in Normandy is plentiful and diverse, from cheap camp sites to five-star hotels in glorious châteaux. However, early booking is advised if you wish to travel between June and August. In the area covered by this book, accommodation is most easily found in Isigny, Carentan, Grandcamp-Maisy and St-Lô. In Isigny the *Hôtel de France* (tel: +33 (0)2 31 22 00 33) offers good accommodation, and the chance to visit the caramel factory in the town, renowned in France and beyond for its dairy produce, and the co-operative dairy itself. The campsite at Isigny has 112 places (tel: +33 (0)2 31 21 33 20). There are many hotels in St-Lô, and you can eat in a wide variety of bistros and restaurants. The *Auberge Normand* offers modest but comfortable rooms and traditional food in an old fashioned atmosphere, or you can visit the *Café Grand Bacon* on the corner of the Place Charles de Gaulle. If you wish to stay near St-Lô but not in town, try *Château de la Roque* (tel: +33 (0)2 33 57 33 20; web: <www.chateau-de-la-roque.fr>). This sixteenth-century château, just off the D900 to the west of Hébécrevon, offers bed, breakfast and dinner in the middle of a park with sporting and leisure facilities. The dinners are served to guests collectively, sitting together at long tables, so be prepared to be sociable.

Soldiers of 29th Infantry Division making use of hard cover, 19 July. The censor has blotted out the divisional badges worn by the troops. *(USNA)*

Useful contacts for accommodation and other information include:

French Travel Centre, 178 Piccadilly, London W1V 0AL;
  tel: 0870 830 2000; web: www.raileurope.co.uk
French Tourist Authority, 444 Madison Avenue, New York,
  NY 10022 (other offices in Chicago, Los Angeles and Miami);
  web: www.francetourism.com
Calvados Tourisme, Place du Canada, 14000 Caen;
  tel: +33 (0)2 31 86 53 30; web: www.calvados-tourisme.com
Manche Tourisme, web: www.manchetourisme.com
Maison du Tourisme de Cherbourg et du Haut-Cotentin,
  2 Quai Alexandre III, 50100 Cherbourg-Octeville;
  tel: +33 (0)2 33 93 52 02; web: www.ot-cherbourg-cotentin.fr
Office de Tourisme de St-Lô, Place du General de Gaulle, St-Lô;
  tel: +33 (0)2 33 77 60 35
Office de Tourisme Isigny-sur-Mer, 1 Rue Victor Hugo, BP 110;
  tel: +33 (0)2 31 21 46 00
Gîtes de France, La Maison des Gîtes de France et du Tourisme
  Vert, 59 Rue Saint-Lazare, 75 439 Paris Cedex 09;
  tel: +33 (0)1 49 70 75 75; web: www.gites-de-france.fr

BATTLEFIELD TOURING

Each volume in the 'Battle Zone Normandy' series contains three or more battlefield tours. These are intended to last from a few hours to a full day apiece. Some are best undertaken using motor transport, others should be done on foot, and many involve a mixture of the two. Owing to its excellent infrastructure and relatively gentle topography, Normandy also makes a good location for a cycling holiday; indeed, some of our tours are ideally suited to this method.

In every case the tour author has visited the area concerned recently, so the information presented should be accurate and reasonably up to date. Nevertheless land use, infrastructure and rights of way can change, sometimes at short notice. If you encounter difficulties in following any tour, we would very much like to hear about it, so we can incorporate changes in future editions. Your comments should be sent to the publisher at the address provided at the front of this book.

To derive maximum value and enjoyment from the tours, we suggest you equip yourself with the following items:

The Château de Colombières (*see Tour A*) is one of the most impressive buildings in the area covered by this book, and is open to visitors on weekday afternoons in July and August. *(ST)*

- Appropriate maps. European road atlases can be purchased from a wide range of locations outside France. However, for navigation within Normandy, the French Institut Géographique National (IGN) produces maps at a variety of scales (www.ign.fr). The 1:100,000 series ('Top 100') is particularly useful when driving over larger distances; sheet 06 (Caen – Cherbourg) covers most of the invasion area. For pinpointing locations precisely, the current IGN 1:25,000 Série Bleue is best (extracts from this series are used for the tour maps in this book). These can be purchased in many places across Normandy. They can also be ordered in the UK from some bookshops, or from specialist dealers such as the Hereford Map Centre, 24–25 Church Street, Hereford HR1 2LR; tel: 01432 266322; web: <www.themapcentre.com>. Allow at least a fortnight's notice, although some maps may be in stock. The Série Bleue sheets required to cover the areas discussed in this book are: 1312E Carentan, 1313E St-Lô, 1412OT Pointe du Hoc and 1413O Torigni-sur-Vire.
- Lightweight waterproof clothing and robust footwear are essential, especially for touring in the countryside.
- Take a compass, provided you know how to use one!

- A camera and spare films/memory cards.
- A notebook to record what you have photographed.
- A French dictionary and/or phrasebook. (English is widely spoken in the coastal area, but is much less common inland.)
- Food and drink. Although you are never very far in Normandy from a shop, restaurant or *tabac*, many of the tours do not pass directly by such facilities. It is therefore sensible to take some light refreshment with you.
- Binoculars. Most officers and some other ranks carried binoculars in 1944. Taking a pair adds a surprising amount of verisimilitude to the touring experience.

SOME DO'S AND DON'TS

Battlefield touring can be an extremely interesting and even

emotional experience, especially if you have read something about the battles beforehand. In addition, it is fair to say that residents of Normandy are used to visitors, among them battlefield tourers, and generally will do their best to help if you encounter problems. However, many of the tours in the 'Battle Zone Normandy' series are off the beaten track, and you can expect some puzzled looks from the locals, especially inland. In all cases we have tried to ensure that tours are on public land, or viewable from public rights of way. However, in the unlikely event that you are asked to leave

The scale of the 60th anniversary commemorations of the Battle of Normandy demonstrated how much interest remains in the struggle that took place here in 1944. This plaque is one of the most recent additions to the 29th Infantry Division memorial near the River Elle (*see also p. 44*). (ST)

a site, do so immediately and by the most direct route.

In addition: **Never remove 'souvenirs' from the battlefields.** Even today it is not unknown for farmers to turn up relics of the 1944 fighting. Taking these without permission may not only be illegal, but can be extremely dangerous. It also ruins the site for genuine battlefield archaeologists. Anyone returning from France should also remember customs regulations on the import of weapons and ammunition of any kind.

BATTLEFIELD TOURS

Be especially careful when investigating fortifications. Some of the more frequently-visited sites are well preserved, and several of them have excellent museums. However, both along the coast and inland there are numerous positions that have been left to decay, and which carry risks for the unwary. In particular, remember that many of these places were the scenes of heavy fighting or subsequent demolitions, which may have caused severe (and sometimes invisible) structural damage. Coastal erosion has also undermined the foundations of a number of shoreline defences. Under no circumstances should underground bunkers, chambers and tunnels be entered, and care should always be taken when examining above-ground structures. If in any doubt, stay away.

Beware of hunting (shooting) areas (signposted *Chasse Gardée*). Do not enter these, even if they offer a short cut to your destination. Similarly, Normandy contains a number of restricted areas (military facilities and wildlife reserves), which should be avoided. Watch out, too, for temporary footpath closures, especially along sections of coastal cliffs.

If using a motor vehicle, keep your eyes on the road. There are many places to park, even on minor routes, and it is always better to turn round and retrace your path than to cause an accident. In rural areas avoid blocking entrances and driving along farm tracks; again, it is better to walk a few hundred metres than to cause damage and offence.

TOURING AROUND ST-LÔ

In St-Lô itself, the Place Charles de Gaulle has a memorial to the civilian victims of the war, and leads on into the heart of the old town, surrounded by restored medieval walls and towers. To the north the church of St-Georges-Montcoq dominates the town. About 100 metres west of the Place Charles de Gaulle is the cathedral of Nôtre Dame, preserved in a semi-ruined condition. In the suburb of la Madeleine is a chapel, with a memorial to 29th and 35th Infantry Divisions. On the D972, at the crossroads with the D6, is a roundabout dedicated to Major Thomas D. Howie, commander of 2/116th, whose body lay in state on the steps of the church at Ste-Croix after being carried into the town by his men.

St-Lô also offers a Museum of the Bocage, and visits to the National Stud. On Thursday afternoons in August there are displays of horses and carriages in the arena. Visit the tourist office (*details on p. 117*) for a comprehensive list of things to see in the area.

Attractions in St-Lô

Bocage Museum: Musée du Bocage Normand, Ferme de Bois Jugan, 50000 St-Lô; tel: +33 (0)2 33 56 26 98; email: <musee.bocage.normand@ wanadoo.fr>. Admission charge.

French National Stud: Haras National de St-Lô, Avenue du Maréchal Juin, BP 360, 50010 St-Lô; tel: +33 (0)2 33 77 88 77; email: <haras.saintlo@ haras-nationaux.fr>. Open for accompanied visits at 1430 and 1730 every day 1 June – 30 Sept, and at 1100, 1 July – 30 Aug. Admission charge.

All the tours in this book start and/or end in either Isigny-sur-Mer or St-Lô. Both are readily accessible from elsewhere in the region. Isigny is just off the N13 road, the main Caen–Cherbourg highway, and now, as in 1944, St-Lô is the focus of numerous major routes.

WAR CEMETERIES

There are two US war cemeteries in Normandy, both of which contain the graves of many American servicemen who died during the battle for St-Lô. The larger and more famous is at Colleville-sur-Mer, overlooking Omaha Beach. It contains 9,386 graves, among them 307 unknown burials. There is also a Garden of the Missing, with a wall upon which are inscribed the names of 1,557 personnel with no known graves. The other US cemetery is near St-James, south of Avranches. A total of 4,410 US soldiers are buried here, with a Wall of the Missing commemorating 498 others. Both cemeteries are within an hour's easy drive of St-Lô.

Details of the German war cemetery at la Cambe, where 21,222 personnel are buried, can be found in Tour A (*p. 122*). There is another German cemetery near Marigny, west of St-Lô (11,169 graves), and a third at Orglandes, between Carentan and Valognes on the Cotentin (10,152 graves).

War Cemeteries

Colleville Military Cemetery, Omaha Beach, Colleville-sur-Mer. The beach and cemetery are easily reached from Isigny-sur-Mer or the N13.

St-James Military Cemetery To reach St-James from St-Lô drive south on the D999 to join the N175 near Villedieu-les-Poêles; continue to Pontaubault and then take the D998 south to St-James.

Further details on both cemeteries can be found at <www.abmc.gov>; both are open to the public 0900–1700 daily, except 25 Dec and 1 Jan.

BATTLEFIELD TOURS

TOUR A

115ᵀᴴ INFANTRY & THE CROSSING OF THE AURE

OBJECTIVE: This tour explores US 115th Infantry Regiment's crossing of the River Aure on 9 June 1944 and its exploitation southwards.

DURATION/SUITABILITY: The tour lasts half a day, or a full day if the optional extras (*see Stands A1, A2 and A4*) are included. The total distance covered is about 35 km, generally along quiet roads after leaving the N13; it is suitable for cyclists. All stands are accessible by car.

Stand A1: Canchy

DIRECTIONS: Leave Isigny on the N13 towards Caen; you are on the axis of advance to Isigny by 175th Infantry Regiment on 8–9 June, but heading in the opposite direction. On the right-hand side you can see the flood plain of the Aure Inférieure, which was inundated with water to waist height in 1944.

To visit the largest German war cemetery (*Deutsches Soldatenfriedhof*) in Normandy, leave the main road at la Cambe, following signs to the cemetery at the roundabout immediately south of the N13. Alternatively, continue on the N13 for 1.5 km beyond la Cambe before turning south onto the D204. Head downhill for 750 metres and turn left at the T-junction onto the D124. After 250 metres take the minor road on your right, which leads into Canchy. Follow the road for 1.25 km until you reach a footbridge over the river. From here you have superb views across the water meadows at almost precisely the point where 115th Infantry Regiment crossed on the morning of 9 June 1944.

THE ACTION: After its bloody baptism of fire on Omaha Beach, 29th Division made rapid progress towards its D-Day objectives on 8 June. While 175th Infantry pushed west to Isigny and 116th Infantry overcame opposition near Grandcamp, in the eastern part of the divisional sector Colonel Eugene Slappey's

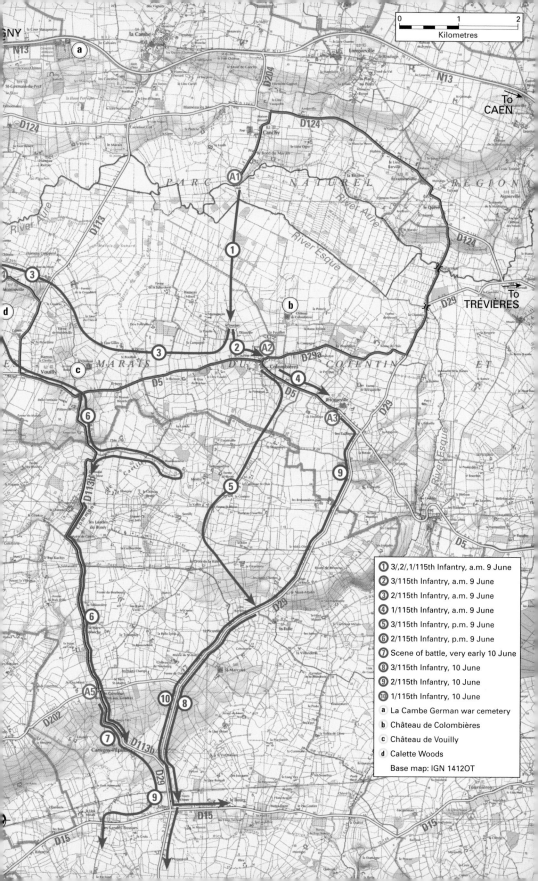

①	3/,2/,1/115th Infantry, a.m. 9 June
②	3/115th Infantry, a.m. 9 June
③	2/115th Infantry, a.m. 9 June
④	1/115th Infantry, a.m. 9 June
⑤	3/115th Infantry, p.m. 9 June
⑥	2/115th Infantry, p.m. 9 June
⑦	Scene of battle, very early 10 June
⑧	3/115th Infantry, 10 June
⑨	2/115th Infantry, 10 June
⑩	1/115th Infantry, 10 June
a	La Cambe German war cemetery
b	Château de Colombières
c	Château de Vouilly
d	Calette Woods
	Base map: IGN 1412OT

115th Infantry advanced towards the Aure. After occupying Deux-Jumeaux and Longueville and dispersing the remaining German defenders, by mid-afternoon the regiment was deployed along the high ground north of the river.

At 2115 hours on 8 June Maj Gen Gerow issued V Corps Field Order No. 2 for an attack by 1st, 2nd and 29th Divisions the following day, to enlarge the beachhead and conform to British XXX Corps' advance east of the River Drôme. In the case of 29th Division, this order confirmed oral instructions already issued to cross the Aure during the night of 8–9 June, with the aim of reaching the River Elle, 12 km north-east of St-Lô, within 24 hours.

The footbridge over the Aure at Canchy, looking south across the flood plain towards Colombières. *(ST)*

During the evening of 8 June naval guns and the 105-mm howitzers of 110th Field Artillery Battalion shelled Colombières, Calette Wood and Bricqueville, which were the initial objectives for 115th Infantry's 3rd, 2nd and 1st Battalions respectively. US patrols also crossed the inundated area to reconnoitre routes for the main assault. Particularly impressive results were achieved by 2nd Lieutenant Kermit C. Miller, who set off from Longueville with 28 men, mainly from E/115th Infantry, on the evening of the 8th. Familiar with the marshlands of Chesapeake Bay, around which many of them were recruited, the Americans discovered a boat and crossed the valley to Colombières. The Germans on the opposite bank, exhausted by the fighting on Omaha and confident of their safety behind such a wide obstacle, were not on the alert, and were swiftly overcome. After relaying news of their achievement by radio, Miller's men returned across the river the following morning, bringing a number of prisoners with them.

> **Lieutenant Miller's Distinguished Service Cross citation provides further details of the patrol:**
>
> 'Reaching Colombières, Lt. Miller was informed by French civilians that a large number of German soldiers were in a nearby building. Tactically disposing his men, he ordered the Germans to surrender but was answered by rifle fire. During the exchange of fire which followed, enemy reinforcements arrived and in the ensuing struggle many of the enemy were killed and wounded and 17 were captured.
>
> Aware that his men required rest, Lt. Miller moved his patrol to another sector of town where they remained in a barn that night. All through the night Lt. Miller was constantly alert, supervising the guard and attending the wounded. The return march the next morning was extremely arduous and difficult; the wounded required constant attention and the prisoners required a close guard.'
>
> *Source:* Joseph Binkoski and Arthur Plaut, *The 115th Infantry Regiment in World War II*, p. 33.

Stand A2: Colombières

DIRECTIONS: Retrace your route to the D124 and turn right to Écrammeville, about 3 km distant. Pass the church on your left and continue through the village, ignoring all junctions with minor roads before heading uphill through the hamlet of le Quévé (which was occupied by 1/115th Infantry on 8 June). Pause at the hilltop calvary for views west and east before turning right here onto a minor road, which heads down to cross the Aure at Pont de l'Acre. At the next T-junction turn right onto the D29 before crossing a second bridge, this time over the River Esque (the tiniest of streams). After about 900 metres turn right again and drive along the D29a for 2 km to Colombières. Note that the Château de Colombières, an exquisite 14th-century moated castle 750 metres north-east of the village, is open to visitors on afternoons during July and August.

THE ACTION: Early on 9 June 115th Infantry began its attack across the Aure. South-east of Écrammeville, 1/115th was held up by fire from Trévières and abandoned its attempt to cross the river. South of Canchy, despite an absence of resistance, 3rd Battalion also ran into problems when deep water stopped further movement. However, rapid work by 121st Engineer Combat Battalion, which used rubber boats and timber to construct 10 improvised foot bridges, opened a route across the worst of the obstacles, and 3/115th continued through the swamp, led by Company K. A bridgehead was established at le Fournay, and by 1020 hours I and L Companies had advanced into Colombières. Following Lt Miller's raid the night before, the village was unoccupied, and 3/115th dug in while the rest of the regiment crossed the Aure behind it.

A plaque on Colombières church, commemorating the liberation of the village by 115th Infantry Regiment. *(ST)*

> **Lieutenant Richard Quigley, 3/115th Infantry, describes the passage across the inundated area:**
>
> 'We crossed many little waterways a few feet wide which were easily over our heads in depth. Men had to help each other to keep from drowning. The best way to cross them was to jump in and grab the rifle offered to you by the man ahead, who had climbed up on the other side. I often wondered how the leading scouts got across them first.'
>
> *Source:* 29th Division combat interviews, RG 407, Box 24014, Folder 81, USNA.

According to orders issued around 1400 hours, 3/115th Infantry was supposed to proceed to la Folie, 4.5 km further south. However, the commanding officer, Major Victor Gillespie, was reluctant to do so before the battalion had received its rations. When Colonel Slappey arrived at the battalion command post, he discovered that the movement had not taken place. He immediately relieved Gillespie, appointing Captain (later Major) Grat Hankins as the new commander. During the evening 3/115th finally pushed forward, reaching la Folie around midnight, where it again dug in.

Stand A3: Bricqueville

DIRECTIONS: Turn left onto the D5 in the centre of Colombières and drive 1.5 km to Bricqueville. Turn left by the war memorial and park beside the church.

Bricqueville church, the bell ropes of which were cut by US troops on 10 June. *(ST)*

THE ACTION: Having failed to cross the Aure between Écrammeville and Trévières, 1/115th followed the route taken by the rest of the regiment, arriving in Colombières before noon on the 9th. From there it advanced south-east along the D5 towards Bricqueville. On the outskirts of the hamlet it encountered determined resistance from German infantry, supported by several armoured vehicles. For a brief period it appeared that counter-attacks might overrun the US troops, but a forward observer from 115th Regiment's Cannon Company called down fire from his unit's 105-mm howitzers emplaced north of the

Aure, and the Germans were thrown back. In close-quarters fighting a Silver Star was won by Private First Class Robert Moore, who attacked a German armoured vehicle with a rifle-grenade in order to rescue some of his comrades from captivity, and by nightfall 1/115th Infantry had reached its objective. The village was secured the following morning, much to the delight of its inhabitants, who celebrated by ringing the church bells. For the attackers, this drawing of attention to their position was thoroughly unwelcome, and they therefore cut the bell ropes before pressing on towards the Elle late on 10 June!

Stand A4: Monfréville church

DIRECTIONS: Return to Colombières along the D5 and bear left at the church (still on the D5). Continue west for about 3.5 km until you reach the crossroads with the D113b on the eastern edge of Vouilly.

Souvenirs of 1944 in the former US Army pressroom in the Château de Vouilly. (Author)

If you have time to do so, turn right (north) onto the D113b and after 500 metres take the right hand fork into the grounds of the Château de Vouilly. This building was home to the American press corps and their military censors in June and July 1944. Here Lt Gen Bradley explained his plans and concepts for Operation 'Cobra' to the reporters and broadcasters. A plaque unveiled in the presence of the famous journalist Walter Cronkite, and exhibits in the old pressroom, commemorate these events. Today the château offers bed and breakfast, with fine elegant rooms, all *en suite*. Madame Hamel is happy to explain the history of the château and its use in 1944. (Château de Vouilly, 14230 Isigny-sur-Mer; tel: +33 (0)2 31 22 08 59; open 1 April to 30 November.)

Otherwise, continue along the D5 through Vouilly (Église) into Vouilly (Mairie). Here, turn right onto the D113 and head north for 1.25 km until you reach a minor road on your left (with a small sign to the *mairie*). Turn onto this road and follow it uphill to Monfréville church. From here you have outstanding views across the flood plain to the positions held by the Americans on the morning of 9 June, and can appreciate the significance of this position for German artillery observers. The Bois de Calette, one of 115th Infantry Regiment's initial objectives, is visible about 500 metres south of the church. The causeway to the north-east was used by 110th Field Artillery Battalion and 115th Regiment's support units to cross the Aure on 10 June, following repair work by V Corps' 254th Engineer Combat Battalion.

View north across the Aure flood plain from Monfréville church, with the D113 causeway visible across the photo. *(ST)*

THE ACTION: With 3/115th Infantry safely established south of the Aure and Esque, the way was clear for 2/115th to cross the inundated area. It did so by 1100 hours on the 9th, and then moved towards the Bois de Calette, encountering fire from German troops near Vouilly. After clearing opposition on the slopes a kilometre west of Monfréville church, the battalion attempted to mop up scattered resistance in the woodland a few hundred metres to the south. Despite two supporting concentrations of artillery, however, not until 1900 hours was the battalion able to turn back through Vouilly towards its next objective, which lay 5 km further south at the crossroads of le Carrefour des Vignes aux Gendres.

Stand A5: le Carrefour des Vignes aux Gendres

DIRECTIONS: Retrace your route to the crossroads with the D113b at Vouilly (Eglise). This time turn right towards Cartigny-l'Épinay, which lies about 7 km to the south.

Le Carrefour des Vignes aux Gendres, looking north. The memorial to the battle can be seen on the left. *(Author)*

Drive carefully along the D113b, crossing the tiny stream of the Ruisseau de la Fontaine Carabin about 750 metres south of the crossroads. As 2/115th Infantry discovered on 9 June 1944, it is quite easy to get lost in this area. However, the modern road signs are good, and apart from a left turn onto the D195 (signposted Bernesq), from which you should turn right again onto the D113b after only 100 metres, there is little reason for confusion. Stay on the D113b until you reach the crossroads with the D202 at le Carrefour des Vignes aux Gendres, about 1 km north of Cartigny-l'Épinay. There is a memorial to the action described below at the crossroads. According to the locals, the fighting actually took place in the valley bottom just north of Cartigny-l'Épinay, to which you should proceed after inspecting the monument.

The view south from the D113b at le Carrefour des Vignes aux Gendres is spectacular and panoramic, and indicates why 2/115th Infantry strove to reach this objective on 9 June. *(ST)*

THE ACTION: Following a wrong turn near Vouilly, which took the battalion almost to Mestry before the error was recognised, 2/115th Infantry advanced south along the D113b during the late evening of 9 June. By now the US troops had covered a great distance, much of it over difficult terrain or under German fire, and most were thirsty, hungry and exhausted. Nevertheless, at about 0100 hours on 10 June they reached le Carrefour, where Major Maurice Clift, the battalion's Executive Officer, had already reconnoitred a bivouac area in the fields about 900 metres south of the crossroads. Gratefully, the men of the leading companies (F, G and H) filed into a pasture (some sources describe it as an orchard) to the right of the road, where most of them slumped to the ground and immediately fell asleep. Meanwhile, elements of the Headquarters Company and E Company waited on the D113b to enter a field to their left.

Private (later Lieutenant) William Lehman, with an artillery liaison section attached to 2/115th Infantry, takes up the story:

'Our jeep was following along at the rear of the 2nd Battalion's foot troops, carrying another member of the section besides myself, about a half-dozen weary infantrymen, the artillery radios and... a mess of equipment that the infantry had tossed on. When the column halted the fellows on the jeep would go back and take up positions behind the jeep as sort of a rear guard.

At one stop we heard the noise of tracked vehicles to the rear. We didn't pay too much attention to it but at the next stop we heard the sound even louder as though the vehicles, whatever they were, were approaching us. We thought they might be some of the Weasels [light amphibious tracked vehicles used by 29th Division's engineers] that had been used during the day to help us cross the inundated area. Finally, as the main part of the column had turned off the main road, we stopped again and it sounded like the sounds came from just to our rear.

One of the men went back to investigate. We heard him call out and then we heard the sound of a burp gun [submachine gun] and a groan. Right after that a machine gun opened up down the road from us and we all hit the dirt. We worked our way down the road to where the main part of the battalion was and found that it had entered a field on the opposite side. We dashed across the road and into the field and just as we got there the Germans opened up with machine guns, mortars and direct fire from tanks. We saw one group of men trying to set up a machine gun but it jammed on the first round.'

Source: Joseph Binkoski and Arthur Plaut, *The 115th Infantry Regiment in World War II*, p. 38.

Almost by chance, 2/115th's soldiers found themselves under heavy attack from a column of armoured vehicles, guns and bicycle-mounted infantry, which had been retreating from the Aure in the wake of the American advance. Unfortunately, the US battalion was in no position to mount an organised defence. Most of the HQ Company officers were killed or wounded at the start of the action, while the battalion commander himself, Lt Col William C. Warfield also died early – apparently while charging a German assault gun, armed only with a pistol. In scenes of utter chaos, and despite some gallant attempts to resist, the American forces splintered into small groups and scattered into the surrounding countryside. Within an hour around 150 of 2/115th's personnel were killed, wounded, or taken prisoner. Among the dead was Lieutenant Miller, whose inspired action less than 24 hours earlier had done so much to open the route for 29th Division's advance.

The battle site, looking south along the D113b towards the church of Cartigny-l'Épinay. According to local inhabitants, the field on the right is the place where 2/115th Infantry had bedded down for the night when it was attacked. *(ST)*

Combat historian Sergeant Forrest Pogue's record of his interview with Major Maurice Clift paints a vivid picture:

'Major [Clift] ducked down behind hedge. 88-mm bounced him off ground. Started across field; Germans started down highway along fence row. Major and Sgt turned back and Germans followed. Dropped in grass. After a time went over to F and G Companies to look for radio. Pvt Armbruster of Company G got one tank [probably an assault gun or self-propelled gun, since the Germans had no tanks in the area] with a bazooka and the ammunition in it blew the first tank up 300 feet and set another tank afire... To get away from Germans men had to crawl towards their own MGs; called to the men and got by safely. Major found E Company. It had no cover in field except a ditch. Found 12 men in a ditch. Sgt from H Company asked what are we to do? Major replied "I don't know". Men began to leave. Major... got some officers together and they had a little council of war... Decided that there was no chance to do anything. There was utter confusion and no chance to organize men. Position not tenable... Majority of the men went elsewhere... Major started back to Bricqueville.'

Source: 29th Division combat interviews, Record group 407, Box 24014, Folder 81, USNA.

Two GIs of 115th Infantry Regiment read *Stars and Stripes*, the US Army newspaper, near Ste-Marguerite-d'Elle, 16 June. *(USNA)*

EPILOGUE: Despite the damage caused to 2/115th overnight, by the evening of 9 June German resistance south of the Aure had been shattered by the speed and tempo of the US advance. Following approval of his request to withdraw, on the morning of the 10th GenLt Kraiss ordered the abandonment of 352nd Division's remaining positions near Trévières (in US 2nd Infantry Division's sector) and pulled his surviving forces back to the River Elle.

On the same day, 3/115th Infantry advanced almost unopposed from la Folie to the high ground overlooking the Elle 2.5 km east of Ste-Marguerite-d'Elle. Meanwhile, after gathering together its scattered elements, it was discovered that 2/115th Infantry had not in fact been destroyed, as initial reports had indicated. Having received over a hundred replacements, plus a new commander (Lt Col Arthur Sheppe) and some tank support, at 1600 hours the battalion moved south again through le Carrefour. By nightfall it had taken up positions a few hundred metres north of Ste-Marguerite-d'Elle. Finally, after consolidating at Bricqueville, 1/115th Infantry also headed south, going into regimental reserve at le Bourg by the end of the day. The regiment then began preparing for a major attack to cross the River Elle, which was to begin on Monday 12 June.

ENDING THE TOUR: You are now well placed to explore 29th Division's crossing of the Elle on 12–13 June (*see pp. 39–44*). Alternatively, to return to Isigny, continue south-east along the D113b until you reach a T-junction with the D29. Turn right (south) for about 600 metres before turning right onto the D15. Follow this road to the T-junction with the D11. Here, turn right and take the D11 north all the way to Isigny.

TOUR B

PANZER LEHR DIVISION'S COUNTER-ATTACK

OBJECTIVE: This tour examines the ground over which Panzer Lehr Division made its unsuccessful counter-attack on 11 July.

DURATION/SUITABILITY: This tour takes about half a day, although there is potential to extend it by visiting other interesting sites in the area. The total distance from Stand B1 to Stand B6 is about 22 km. The tour is suitable for those with mobility difficulties. Most of the roads (other than the N174) are quiet, and the tour can also therefore be undertaken by bicycle.

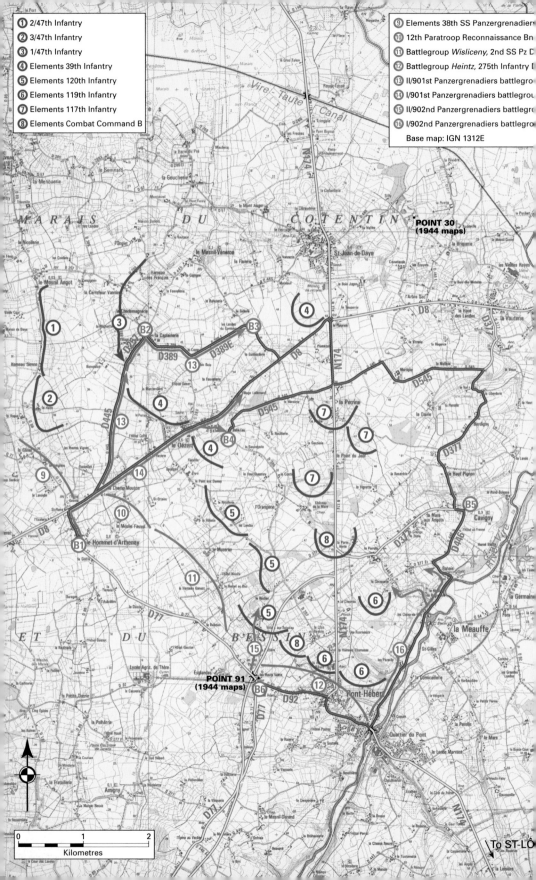

① 2/47th Infantry
② 3/47th Infantry
③ 1/47th Infantry
④ Elements 39th Infantry
⑤ Elements 120th Infantry
⑥ Elements 119th Infantry
⑦ Elements 117th Infantry
⑧ Elements Combat Command B
⑨ Elements 38th SS Panzergrenadiers
⑩ 12th Paratroop Reconnaissance Bn
⑪ Battlegroup *Wisliceny*, 2nd SS Pz D
⑫ Battlegroup *Heintz*, 275th Infantry D
⑬ II/901st Panzergrenadiers battlegro
⑭ I/901st Panzergrenadiers battlegrou
⑮ II/902nd Panzergrenadiers battlegro
⑯ I/902nd Panzergrenadiers battlegro
Base map: IGN 1312E
Vire - Taute Canal
MARAIS DU COTENTIN
ET DU BESSIN
POINT 30 (1944 maps)
POINT 91 (1944 maps)
St-Jean-de-Daye
le Mesnil-Véneron
le Mesnil Angot
le Dézert
le Hommet-d'Arthenay
Cavigny
la Meauffe
Pont-Hébert
Quartier du Pont
la Perrine
B1
B2
B3
B4
B5
B6
D8
D77
D92
D174
D377
D389
D389E
D445
D446
D545
N174
0 1 2
Kilometres
To ST-LÔ

Stand B1: le Hommet-d'Arthenay

DIRECTIONS: Leave the centre of Isigny on the D197A heading west, more or less parallel with the N13 to the south. Cross the River Vire and then turn left onto the D444 at the crossroads in la Blanche. Follow the road for 3.25 km into l'Enauderie, held by Battlegroup *Heintz* against US troops on 12 June, and the scene of heavy fighting on the 15th (*see pp. 57–8*).

The view south-west along the D8 from le Dézert. I/901st Panzergrenadiers' battlegroup approached the village along this road, but was repulsed by US troops, backed by artillery and air attacks by fighter-bombers. *(Author)*

Continue for 600 metres towards Montmartin-en-Graignes. At the calvary on the western edge of the village bear right, and after 800 metres you will reach the N174, the main arterial route west of the Vire. Turn left and drive 3 km to the Vire–Taute Canal. Cross the canal, scene of the assault crossing by 120th Infantry on 7 July (*see p. 68*), and continue 2 km into St-Jean-de-Daye. Pass through the town to a roundabout 500 metres beyond its southern outskirts. This is le Fleurion, 30th Infantry Division's first objective on 7 July. Turn right onto the D8, approaching le Dézert (le Désert on 1944 maps) after about 2 km. This was the route of 120th Infantry's advance on 8 July. Heavy fighting took place during this phase of the attack. Reports of German reinforcements arriving north of St-Lô also caused Maj Gen Corlett, XIX Corps' commander, to become concerned about the possibility of a major counter-attack. To strengthen the American drive, on 9 July elements of VII Corps' 9th Infantry Division crossed into the bridgehead north of St-Jean-de-Daye. Simultaneously, the D8 became the boundary between 9th Division's 39th Infantry Regiment and 30th Division's 120th Infantry, which shifted its axis to the left, along the modern D389.

Continue through le Dézert, captured by 39th Infantry Regiment on 10 July. At the crossroads with the D77 turn left and stop near the church in le Hommet-d'Arthenay.

A camouflaged Panther, with two panzergrenadiers on its engine deck, prepares to go into action. Tank and infantry teams like these formed the main component of Panzer Lehr's attack on 11 July. *(BA 1011-301-1955-22)*

THE ACTION: Panzer Lehr Division's 901st Panzergrenadier Regiment battlegroup assembled here on 10 July. Its two under-strength infantry battalions, reinforced with around 30 Panther tanks from I/6th Panzer Regiment and some halftrack-mounted cannon and flamethrowers, had orders to strike north-east along the D8 and the D445. The objective was the N174 at St-Jean-de-Daye and Point 30 (the modern Point 44), 1.25 km east of the town. Further divisional elements waited in reserve behind 901st Panzergrenadiers, and flanking units were also placed under Panzer Lehr's tactical control. These included 12th Paratroop Reconnaissance Battalion, immediately east of the D8, and Battlegroup *Wisliceny* (I/3rd SS Panzergrenadier Regiment, from 2nd SS Panzer Division) to its right.

The attack began at 0145 hours on 11 July. The 901st Panzer-grenadiers' battlegroup pushed along the D8 and part of it broke through 39th Infantry Regiment at le Dézert. *En route* a column swung north onto the D445 towards le Mesnil-Véneron, while a flank guard moved along the D545 in the direction of la Perrine. If successful, these manoeuvres would have cut the N174 in three places. Many of the German troops went through the weakest place in 9th Infantry Division's line, between 47th and 39th Infantry Regiments. Here, owing to the extension of 47th Infantry's front towards the Bois du Hommet, a gap of 1,600 metres existed in the US positions, covered only by a single rifle company. Consequently, little resistance was offered to the Germans, who overran 3/47th's command post and aid station as they advanced north.

Stand B2: la Caplainerie

DIRECTIONS: Retrace your route to the D8 and turn right. About 500 metres north-east of the D77/D8 crossroads turn left onto the D445, signposted le Mesnil-Véneron. Follow the road, which becomes the D257 after 1.25 km, to the crossroads at la Caplainerie. This was the route taken by *Major* Schöne's II/901st Panzer-grenadiers, plus around a dozen Panther tanks, in the opening stages of Panzer Lehr's attack.

View south along the D257 just north of la Caplainerie. Although it is impossible to be sure, this may be the site of the engagement described on p. 141. *(ST)*

BATTLEFIELD TOURS

THE ACTION: Having passed through the US front line, II/901st Panzergrenadiers reached la Caplainerie at about 0245 hours. Owing to a failure of co-ordination, the crossroads itself was undefended. However, German reconnaissance 200 metres to the north quickly revealed a blocking position occupied by four M10 tank destroyers (from 3rd Platoon, C Company, 899th Tank Destroyer Battalion – 3/C/899th). Although these were brought under small arms fire, they refused to withdraw. Consequently, part of II/901st's column turned right along the D389 in an attempt to outflank the US position and maintain momentum towards St-Jean-de-Daye.

M10 tank destroyers like this one, passing through St-Fromond on 7 July, played a central role in halting Panzer Lehr Division's assault. Although the M10's open-topped turret made it vulnerable to infantry or artillery attack, and its 3-inch gun lacked penetrating power, at the short ranges at which the fighting took place on 11 July the M10 was able to inflict significant losses on the German spearheads. *(USNA)*

As is explained at Stand B3, the German advance along this axis stalled 2 km further down the road, at la Sellerie. Probably for this reason, at about 1000 hours the Germans renewed their attack northwards from la Caplainerie. However, despite heavy artillery support, by now the Americans were fully alert to the threat to their positions. When a Panther pushed along the road towards le Mesnil-Véneron, it was quickly knocked out by an M10 from an ambush position near the crossroads.

> **Sergeant Hershall Briles (3/C/899th Tank Destroyer Battalion) describes the destruction of the German tank:**
>
> '[The Panther] looked like a piece of the hedgerow as it moved forward... It had camouflage all over it, and it was difficult to tell that it was a tank. My crew had a round of HE [high explosive] in the breech. We shot that at it, and strangely enough it penetrated the thick armour on the left front of the turret. The blast blew off all the camouflage and gave us a clearer target for our next round of AP [armour piercing]. The AP went through at a point about two feet below where the HE had struck. That's because we used the same range and deflection but the AP round is heavier.'
>
> *Source:* 899th Tank Destroyer Battalion records, RG 407, Box 24205, Folder 1055, USNA.

Once the isolation of 3/47th Infantry became known, 9th Infantry Division also took steps to restore connections and to cut off and destroy German forces behind the US front. At 0850 hours 1/47th Infantry, in reserve near le Mesnil-Véneron, was ordered to move south along the D289, west of the village of la Charlemagnerie. The battalion was reinforced with four tank destroyers from 899th Battalion's C Company. Orders were also issued to elements of 3rd Armored Division's 32nd Armored Regiment, in reserve near la Caplainerie, to support the advance south.

Heavy fighting erupted again in the afternoon, as continued attempts by the II/901st battlegroup to push north met US formations moving in the opposite direction. Warned by aircraft of a renewed thrust towards la Caplainerie, Sherman tanks from 32nd Armored Regiment prepared to repulse the Germans from orchards on both sides of the D445. Meanwhile, two M10s from C/899th Tank Destroyer Battalion held their original position north of the crossroads, and 1/47th Infantry closed in from the west.

Two disabled Panthers near le Dézert, possibly those described by Captain Cohen. Note the sloped front glacis plates, which made many anti-tank rounds ricochet off the Panther. *(USNA)*

Captain Abraham Cohen, commanding 32nd Armored Regiment's F Company, described what happened next:

'... word reached Captain Cohen that eight [Panthers] were approaching up the road. Company F saw seven of these very shortly afterwards, and then another one behind this first group. From that time on, Capt. Cohen admits a maze of confusion resulted. He knows that Company F opened up on the enemy armor at a 400 yard range, using HE. The platoon on the east side of the road, which had no field of fire, simply poured HE on the road. Coincidental with the developing tank fight, American aircraft came down on the Panthers, bombing and strafing, while infantrymen in the advance of the 1st Battalion of the 47th arrived on the scene and opened fire with bazookas. The Panthers kept rolling, and one of them fought a point-blank duel with the Tank Destroyers [a fact confirmed by 899th Tank Destroyer Battalion's account, which claimed two Panthers destroyed]... But it was getting too hot for the Panthers. They attempted to extricate themselves from the deadly fire pocket into which they had advanced. Two of them, trying to turn on that narrow road, side-slipped into ditches and were unable to move. Another one was knocked out by bazooka fire… all of the Panthers were destroyed.'

Source: 3rd Armored Division combat interviews, RG 407, Box 24088, Folder 259, USNA.

The D445 to la Caplainerie. Fritz Bayerlein, Panzer Lehr's commander, remarked that his large and heavy Panther tanks, with their long gun barrels, were less suited to *bocage* fighting than his opponents' smaller and more agile vehicles. The events of 11 July indicate that he was correct. *(Author)*

Soon afterwards, 1/47th succeeded in making contact with 3/47th Infantry. The accompanying tank destroyers also knocked out three more Panthers and a troop carrier along the D445. By 1600 hours the German attack had been contained and by 2100 hours 9th Infantry Division's forward battalions were digging in along the line they had occupied on 10 July. At least on the western axis, Panzer Lehr's counter-attack had been brought to a complete halt.

Before leaving la Caplainerie, walk south along the D257/D445 for 200 metres. On the left-hand side is an orchard. This is where some of 32nd Armored Regiment's Shermans were deployed on 11 July. Continue to the fork with the D289, and then return to appreciate the ambush site from the Germans' point of view.

BATTLEFIELD TOURS

Stand B3: la Sellerie

DIRECTIONS: Turn right (east) at the la Caplainerie crossroads onto the D389. After about 900 metres, where the road forks, bear left on the D389E. After 1 km, stop at another fork in the road 250 metres south-east of la Sellerie. The route you have just followed was taken by part of the II/901st Panzergrenadiers battlegroup early on 11 July, bringing it to within 1.25 km of the N174.

The D389E to la Sellerie, looking north-east from the junction with the D389. II/901st Panzergrenadiers' battlegroup was caught here by US aircraft and tank destroyers on 11 July, and suffered heavy losses. *(ST)*

THE ACTION: The German column (according to US accounts composed of one Panzer IV, 10 Panthers and at least four large half-tracks) reached the road fork immediately south-east of la Sellerie without meeting any opposition. However, here it encountered 3/A/899th Tank Destroyer Battalion, which engaged the Germans at the junction. In the darkness it was impossible to identify targets accurately, and both sides fired at the other's muzzle flashes. Although one M10 was destroyed, so was the leading panzer. This brought the attack temporarily to a halt, and when daylight arrived the Germans found themselves strung out along an exposed section of the road. The Americans took advantage by carrying out air attacks using P-47 fighter-bombers, which inflicted further casualties on the German column.

After withdrawing to Malsoeuf to re-organise, the remaining tank destroyers counter-attacked during the morning. They were joined by several Sherman tanks, along with part of 39th Infantry Regiment. Despite attempts by panzergrenadiers to stop them, additional troops from 3/39th Infantry also redeployed to the la Buhoterie–la Sellerie area to block the road. Passing the la Sellerie fork, one M10 turned onto the track a few hundred metres further south. From near here it engaged three Panthers on the D389E, knocking them out by hits to their side or rear. An armoured half-track which was leading the column was also destroyed. With the German advance stalled, the action then shifted to the la Caplainerie area, as described at Stand B2.

Stand B4: Belle-Eau

DIRECTIONS: Turn right at the road fork and after 750 metres turn left back onto the D8. Drive 1 km to le Fleurion roundabout and turn right (south) onto the N174. Continue south, and immediately after entering la Perrine turn right onto a small, unsigned road (actually the D545). After 2 km you will reach the buildings and twin bridges at Belle-Eau.

The twin bridges at Belle-Eau, looking west along the D545. The leading Panthers of I/901st Panzergrenadiers' battlegroup appeared along the road on the left of the photo, heading towards the camera position. *(ST)*

THE ACTION: Belle-Eau was the scene of another clash on 11 July. Here, four M10s from 1/A/899th Tank Destroyer Battalion engaged part of I/901st's battlegroup at about 0300 hours. One Panther was destroyed, with several others damaged when flames from the burning tank illuminated the scene; one M10 was knocked out. US artillery fire and air attacks then rained down on the D8. According to one account, of 244 panzergrenadiers and 10 Panthers in this column, only 30 men (among them four tank crewmen) regained the German lines at the end of the day.

Stand B5: Cavigny

DIRECTIONS: Retrace your route from Belle-Eau to the N174 at la Perrine. At la Perrine continue straight ahead on the D545, heading east past Martigny and la Mullerie. About 2.5 km east of the N174 you will come to a T-junction with the D377. Turn right, following the road south. You are now following the route of CC B and 119th Infantry's advance on 8 July (*see pp. 70–2*).

View towards the high ground north of the churchyard at Cavigny, with the D377 in the centre. *(Author)*

Continue south for 2.5 km via the dominating ground at le Haut Pignon, occupied by 119th Infantry on the evening of 8 July. On entering Cavigny turn left and park by the church; the churchyard offers a fine view back to the north and le Haut Pignon.

THE ACTION: On 9–10 July 119th Infantry made further progress towards Pont-Hébert from Cavigny. However, stiff resistance from Battlegroup *Heintz* stopped the US troops north of the town on the 10th, and early the next morning they were struck by Panzer Lehr's right-hand column. This included *Major* Kuhnow's I/902nd Panzergrenadiers and about ten Panzer IVs from 8th Company, 130th Panzer Regiment (8/130th). Their objective was the Vire crossing at St-Fromond, about 2.5 km east of 901st Panzergrenadiers' target at Point 44. Considerable firepower, estimated by the Americans as five artillery battalions plus a battery of 88-mm guns, supported the attack.

The German force pushed through the left of 3/119th Infantry along the river road under cover of darkness. By 0930 hours the leading elements were at la Coquerie, west of Bahais. 1/119th Infantry, in reserve south of Cavigny, and 3rd Armored Division's Task Force Y (F/ and I/33rd Armored Regiment, plus A/36th Armored Infantry) moved to intercept them. By 1045 hours the panzers had been halted at Bahais by the M10s of 823rd Tank Destroyer Battalion. Task Force Y then advanced south along the D446, losing six Shermans to fire from self-propelled guns across the Vire. Other elements of the task force swung through la Coquerie to take the Germans in the left flank. The 902nd battlegroup fell back at 1500 hours, and set up strongpoints in Pont-Hébert to block a further American advance. The US troops followed, regaining lost ground.

Stand B6: les Hauts Vents

DIRECTIONS: From Cavigny church take the D446 south. After 1 km turn left to descend to the Vire valley at Bahais. Head south along the river road, reaching Pont-Hébert after about 2.5 km. Turn right onto the N174 by the church and after 800 metres turn left onto the D92 (signposted to le Hommet-d'Arthenay). Follow the road for 1 km to the roadside cross at les Hauts Vents. This was marked as Point 91 on 1944 maps, but as a more modest 73 metres on the current IGN map. Look across the adjacent bridge for spectacular views over the countryside to the west.

Note: Just beyond the cross is a deep cutting, through which the new Pont-Hébert road by-pass runs. If you wish to visit la Rocher, cross the bridge over the bypass and turn right onto the D377, signposted Cavigny.

THE ACTION: After more than 72 hours of exhausting fighting, much of it in the rain, by the end of 10 July elements of 120th Infantry Regiment and CC B were closing in on the high ground at les Hauts Vents. About 1 km north of the crossroads, Lt Col Paul McCollum's 3/120th Infantry dug in around the hamlet of le Rocher. Roadblocks were set up to control the most likely approaches, and tanks and M10s patrolled forward as darkness fell.

At about 0130 hours on 11 July reports began to arrive at McCollum's command post of German tanks and infantry moving into the battalion's positions. These were elements of Panzer Lehr's II/902nd Panzergrenadiers battlegroup, which included 7/130th Panzer Regiment's Panzer IVs and a company of engineers. This column was the central thrust in Panzer Lehr's counter-attack towards St-Jean-de-Daye. Quickly, the American companies were alerted and a violent close-quarter battle erupted in the confusion of half-light and hedgerows.

Bahais, looking east across the River Vire (just visible centre left). This was the most northerly point reached by I/902nd Panzergrenadiers' battlegroup on 11 July. *(Author)*

Lieutenant Tuttle, 120th Infantry Regiment's historian, describes the action:

'... a German tank had eased up by short advances to within a few yards of the battalion CP [Command Post]. Another was not far behind it and a third was farther

Looking south-west from les Hauts Vents. This panoramic view of the country gave the feature its great tactical value. However, only after Panzer Lehr Division's attack collapsed on 11 July could the Americans secure this position. *(Author)*

down the road near the roadblock, with an armored car behind this last tank. The men in and around the lead tank could be heard conversing in German. One man, believed to be a German officer, was standing in the turret of the tank and attempting to send a radio message.

Lt. Pritchard opened up with his .30-calibre machine gun which was mounted on a jeep and located just inside the CP area. This… acted as a signal for the other men to go to work on the first tank. Pvt. Talarico (3rd Battalion HQ), manning his bazooka alone, fired at it from the front and then through the hedgerow on the side. A bazooka team from Company L [also] opened up on it… Captain McCullough and Captain Shaeffer were tossing hand grenades in the turret and at the Germans in the road. The Germans began screaming for mercy as the tank burst into flame. It made an effort to back up but did not move far.

The Germans behind the tank ran down to the next one to warn them, but our men were upon them with bazookas, hand grenades, pistols, rifle-grenades and machine guns. Captain McCullough, finding himself without a weapon, grabbed a light machine gun from someone and, throwing the belt of ammunition over his shoulder, went after the third tank and the armored car. This third tank managed to get away by backing around a house… The armored car was completely burned up. It became immobile in the mud and was caught there by our men.'

Source: 30th Infantry Division combat interviews, RG 407, Box 24037, Folder 94, USNA.

Although fighting continued for several hours, by mid-morning the German attack had been broken, with five Panzer IVs and four armoured cars destroyed, and 60 prisoners taken. Later in the afternoon, the Americans took advantage of the confusion by launching their own attack towards les Hauts Vents. Spearheaded by CC B's Task Force Z, this quickly carried forward beyond the crossroads. US reinforcements then advanced, establishing defensive positions south and west of this critical position before nightfall.

ENDING THE TOUR: To return to Isigny, retrace your route to the N174 and drive north for 18 km to join the N13 about 8.5 km west of Isigny. Alternatively, to visit St-Lô, follow the N174 south from Pont-Hébert for about 6 km.

TOUR C

THE ATTACK ON HILL 192

OBJECTIVE: This tour examines 2nd Infantry Division's capture of Hill 192, the dominating feature east of St-Lô, on 11 July.

DURATION/SUITABILITY: The tour covers a total distance of 6 km (from Stand C1 to Stand C9) and lasts at least half a day. It is suitable for cyclists but less so for those with mobility difficulties, though much can be seen from a car.

Stand C1: Hameau Roux

DIRECTIONS: Starting from St-Lô, take the D6 towards Isigny. After 4 km turn right onto the D448 ('Captain Carter Road') at les Forges, scene of heavy fighting in mid-June and again at the end

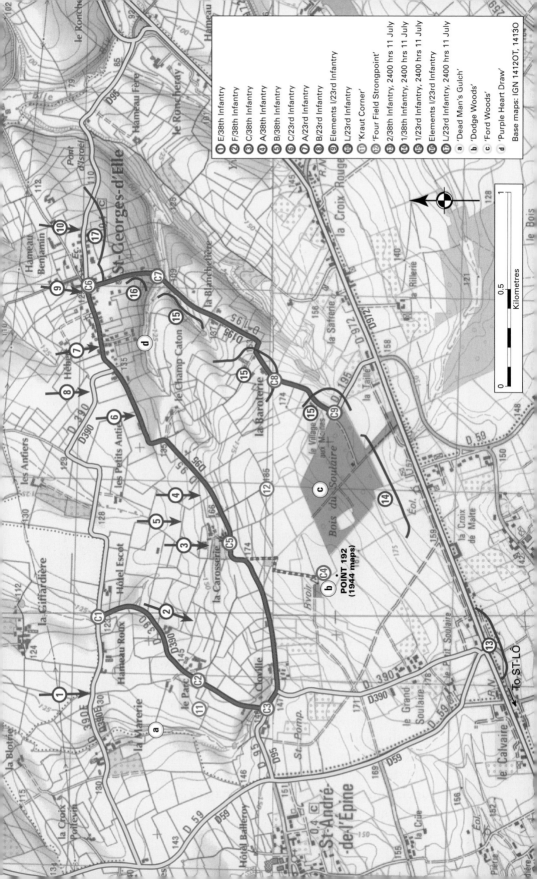

Legend (key):

① E/38th Infantry
② F/38th Infantry
③ C/38th Infantry
④ A/38th Infantry
⑤ B/38th Infantry
⑥ C/23rd Infantry
⑦ A/23rd Infantry
⑧ B/23rd Infantry
⑨ Elements I/23rd Infantry
⑩ L/23rd Infantry
⑪ 'Kraut Corner'
⑫ 'Four Field Strongpoint'
⑬ 2/38th Infantry, 2400 hrs 11 July
⑭ 1/38th Infantry, 2400 hrs 11 July
⑮ 1/23rd Infantry, 2400 hrs 11 July
⑯ Elements I/23rd Infantry
⑰ L/23rd Infantry, 2400 hrs 11 July

a 'Dead Man's Gulch'
b 'Dodge Woods'
c 'Ford Woods'
d 'Purple Heart Draw'

Base maps: IGN 1412OT, 1413O

Kilometres
0   0.5   1

of the month. Travel east along the D448 for 3 km and then turn right onto the D59. After 1 km turn left onto the D390E and continue for 1.75 km, crossing the Ruisseau de Branche at la Marerie. Park your car on the grass verge beside the junction with the D390 at Hameau Roux.

You are now in the area through which Lt Col Jack Norris' 2/38th Infantry Regiment attacked on the morning of 11 July. As a result of earlier fighting, the battalion's front line ran roughly north–south in this sector, along the east bank of the Ruisseau de Branche ('Dead Man's Gulch') down to the D390E. South of the D390E, III/9th Paratroop Regiment occupied several strongpoints on the slopes of Hill 192. One of the most significant lay a few hundred metres south of this stand, at le Parc; a position known to the Americans as 'Kraut Corner'.

Stand C1, looking east along the D390E with the D390 turn on the right. *(ST)*

THE ACTION: According to 2nd Infantry Division's plan, the task of capturing Hill 192 was allocated to Colonel Ralph Zwicker's 38th Infantry Regiment, reinforced by two companies of Shermans and a company of light tanks from 741st Tank Battalion, plus some engineers. It would be assisted by 23rd Infantry Regiment on its left, near St-Georges-d'Elle and Bérigny, and by 9th Infantry Regiment, carrying out diversionary operations on the division's left flank. Massive fire support, including a preliminary bombardment and a rolling barrage to accompany the attack, was provided. H-Hour for 38th Regiment's attack was 0630 hours.

2/38th's attack actually began at H-30 minutes, when E Company moved forward east of the Ruisseau de Branche to bring itself level with F Company, which was deployed astride the D390 between Hameau Roux and Hôtel Escot. E Company (with attached heavy weapons from H Company) attacked with two platoons forward, 2nd on the right and 1st on the left; 3rd Platoon was in reserve. F Company (also reinforced by part of H Company) began its own attack at 0630 hours. Owing to its heavy casualties on 16 June and relative unfamiliarity with the terrain, G Company remained in reserve throughout the day, although this did not prevent it from suffering losses of 5 killed and 2 wounded to German mortar and artillery fire.

View west from le Parc farm across 'Dead Man's Gulch', looking towards the slopes leading to St-André-de-l'Épine. 29th Infantry Division's 116th Regiment attacked through the fields in the distance. *(Author)*

Stand C2: le Parc (Kraut Corner)

DIRECTIONS: Head south along the D390 for 600 metres, passing one cluster of buildings before reaching another shortly afterwards, with a small sign identifying this hamlet as le Parc. Kraut Corner, which commanded the route into the village of Cloville, was in the fields to the right of the road, on the eastern bank of the Ruisseau de Branche (the far bank of which is visible from the roadside near this stand).

THE ACTION: In an attempt to gain information about German dispositions, Kraut Corner was raided on 6 July by a 14-man patrol led by Lieutenant Ralph Winstead. On 11 July the position was heavily shelled by US artillery before 2/38th's attack began. As elsewhere along the front, the effect was devastating.

> *Gefreiter* (Corporal) Helmut Kasiacka, from 10/9th Para-troop Regiment, endured the assault. Later in July a letter describing the bombardment was found on his body:
>
> 'At 0500 hours our Company sector got such a dense hail of artillery and mortar fire, that we thought the world was coming to an end... It scared the pants off us. We could expect a very juicy attack. If we thought the artillery fire had reached its climax we were disillusioned at 0530. At that time a tremendous firing started which continued until 0615... On that day I escaped death just by seconds a hundred times. A piece of shrapnel penetrated through the leather strap of my machine gun and was thus diverted from my chest... At that moment I lost my nerves. I chewed up a cigarette, bit into the ground and acted like a madman... [This was] the most terrible and most gruesome day of my life.'
>
> *Source:* 2nd Infantry Division combat interviews, RG 407, Box 24014, Folder 12, USNA.

Despite its intensity, however, some of the paratroopers survived the bombardment and offered determined resistance to E/38th. US troops also came under heavy pre-registered mortar fire as they approached the strongpoint. E Company's 2nd Platoon was brought to a halt, and although 3rd Platoon moved up on its right to within a few metres of the position, attempts to use grenades to suppress it failed – as the after-action report recorded, some of the defenders 'impudently caught the grenades in pillows and boomeranged them back to the American side of the hedgerow.'

Kraut Corner finally fell when E Company's 1st Platoon worked around the left of the position, supported by some Shermans from B/741st Tank Battalion. Scouts went forward, covered by BARs, machine guns and light mortars. According to the battle narrative, the 'supporting tanks fired so continuously that they sounded like threshing machines.' Then about ten riflemen charged the strong-point, bursting into it from the east. At this point some 15 Germans surrendered, although others continued fighting. Three paratroops, firing from concealed dugouts, were buried alive by one of the trio of tank-dozers supporting 2/38th Infantry. After spending an hour clearing the position, E/38th then moved on towards Cloville.

Bocage country beside the D390, looking east. It was through these fields that F/38th and elements of E/38th Infantry moved south to outflank 'Kraut Corner' and reach their objectives on the D972. *(ST)*

The Germans fought fanatically, even when seriously wounded. One paratrooper in 2/38th's sector caused particular problems:

'A shell had blown off both his legs. American medics approached him, but were fired on by the Schmeisser pistol which he still held in his hand. For several hours he lay in a ditch, firing on whoever approached. Finally he was rescued [*sic*] after our medics sneaked up on him. At the battalion aid station he swore loudly and refused any American aid. Several German medics who were assisting with the treatment of wounded prisoners tried to reason with this paratrooper, but he arrogantly refused treatment.

"He was really a die-hard and he died hard right there in the battalion aid station", says Captain Hugh Mayfield, 2nd Battalion's surgeon.'

Source: 2nd Infantry Division combat interviews, RG 407, Box 24014, Folder 12, USNA.

Stand C3: Cloville

DIRECTIONS: Continue along the D390 for 500 metres to the junction with the D95 at Cloville. Pull over on the verge and look back along the D390, noting how vehicles appearing around the road bend a short distance away would be silhouetted against the skyline, and thus highly vulnerable to fire from this position.

View from the Cloville road junction, looking north along the D390. The vulnerability of vehicles appearing on the skyline in the centre of the photo is obvious. *(ST)*

THE ACTION: Cloville had been shelled by the Americans, and was in ruins when E/38th arrived at around 0930 hours. As at Kraut Corner, however, the paratroops had taken cover in tunnels during the bombardment, and were determined to fight. They were assisted by a Panzer IV and a self-propelled 88-mm gun, both located at the road junction where you are now standing.

Despite the strength of the German position, after a short duel a Sherman commanded by Staff Sergeant Paul Reagan knocked out the German vehicles and E Company entered Cloville. By 1100 the

Americans had mopped up resistance in the village, and were pushing south towards their battalion's objective on the D972 highway. However, at 1245 hours E Company's 2nd Platoon was pinned down by fire from the right rear, in 29th Division's sector. Contact patrols were despatched by 2nd Reconnaissance Troop, and – to quote the battle narrative – 2nd Platoon 'shook off the opposition from the rear by running away from it.' E/38th then advanced quickly, by-passing le Grand Soulaire and reaching the main road east of le Calvaire at around 1700 hours. Here the company dug in, ready to defend against German counter-attacks.

Stand C4: Hill 192

DIRECTIONS: Proceed east along the D95. After about 800 metres you will reach a 90-degree bend in the road. This was the boundary between 38th Infantry's 2nd and 1st Battalions on 11 July. Park beside the road and walk uphill along the track to your right, which turns sharp right before bearing back uphill. Continue for a few hundred metres until you reach a communications mast beside a small building. A short distance to your front left is the western corner of the Bois du Soulaire, or 'Ford Woods' as it was known to the Americans in July 1944. On the way up you can enjoy superb views to the north-west, back over 2/38th's axis of advance.

Ford Woods, looking south-east from Stand C4. *(ST)*

This view north from Hill 192 demonstrates clearly the tactical significance of this critical terrain feature. *(ST)*

The wonderful fields of view available to the defenders of Hill 192 are described in the US after-action report:

'When they reached the crest of the hill, the tired doughboys turned and looked back towards the north; they received a cold shock to see the waters of the English Channel beyond Omaha Beach, and to look down the Elle River valley to Isigny and the Channel beyond. [*Author's note:* This may just be possible in very clear conditions, with binoculars.] From Hill 192 they could see everything they had accomplished in the preceding five weeks – places they had bivouacked, key road nets they had utilized, the Forêt de Cerisy, and virtually every corner of St-Georges-d'Elle for which they had fought bitterly.'

Source: 2nd Infantry Division combat interviews, RG 407, Box 24014, Folder 12, USNA.

THE ACTION: After beginning its attack at 0630 hours, F/38th made steady progress against fragmentary opposition. The company moved through the fields between le Parc and la Carosserie, crossing the D95 at around 0900. Half an hour later the left-hand platoon was in Dodge Woods, which it cleared without difficulty. As Lt Col Norris stated, 'It was just a matter of going in frontally and pushing them out.' Strongpoints in hedge corners were suppressed by artillery, and machine guns with the flanking assault squads took over when the barrage moved on. The sheer weight of fire did the trick. At 1653 hours Norris ordered his mortars to displace forward to a position just west of Dodge Woods, while F Company continued downhill towards the D972. By 1700 the first elements of F/38th had crossed the highway, where they were joined by some Shermans from 741st Tank Battalion. Anti-tank weapons and machine guns were deployed, and by nightfall 2/38th was securely in position, having achieved all its objectives for the day. The battalion's losses on 11 July were 20 killed and 82 wounded.

Stand C5: la Carosserie

DIRECTIONS: Retrace your steps to the D95 and turn right along the road. According to US reports, in 1944 the D95 was a 'typical, narrow rock-surfaced lane about 15 feet wide, with some absent-minded stretches of tar surface here and there.' The road had also been mined by the Germans as part of their defences of Hill 192. Stop after 200 metres by the orientation table on the left-hand side, above la Carosserie farm.

You are now standing on the line of departure for Lt Col Frank Mildren's 1/38th Infantry, supported on 11 July by A/741st Tank Battalion, one company of 4.2-inch mortars and a platoon of engineers. La Carosserie marks the approximate point where C Company crossed the road, with A Company on its left, further east. Each company was reinforced with a platoon of heavy weapons from D Company, with B Company initially in reserve. The main German opposition in this sector came from a position known as the 'Four Fields Strongpoint', manned by two platoons of infantry. Although it is impossible to be certain of its location, this resistance nest appears to have been south of the D95, near Ford Woods in the area attacked by A/38th.

THE ACTION: 1/38th started to move to its forming-up area at 0300 hours, after a harassing bombardment which some soldiers feared might indicate that the attack had been compromised, but which stopped just before movement began. 3/38th covered the front to the south, but withdrew after Mildren's men reached the assembly area north of la Carosserie. By 0415 hours the companies were ready, 400 metres from the line of departure.

A and C Companies moved off at 0620 hours, and crossed the D95 at 0655. The advance was not without difficulty, for some Germans had followed 3/38th Infantry as it withdrew into the artillery safety zone, but the first determined resistance was encountered along the road. Here, pre-registered artillery and mortar fire rained down on the Americans. All six of the Shermans accompanying the first wave were knocked out by a combination of mines, anti-tank weapons and shells. However, the infantry continued moving forward on their own, pushing up the slopes of the hill towards the Bois du Soulaire.

Looking north from the D95 at la Carosserie, with the fields in which 1/38th assembled before its assault in the middle distance. *(Author)*

Despite the lack of tank support, the new hedgerow tactics proved effective:

'Each hedgerow was taken the same methodical way – light mortars, light and heavy machine guns were arranged along one hedgerow to pepper the succeeding hedgerow, while scouts went out the sides, and as the BAR men supported, the riflemen gradually worked their way up to close with the enemy. Some fields were harder than others because they were longer, or because the Germans got the jump in the fire fight.'

Source: 2nd Infantry Division combat interviews, RG 407, Box 24014, Folder 12, USNA.

Unsurprisingly, the toughest resistance came from the Four Fields strongpoint, which could not be reduced despite repeated attacks by A Company. With a gap emerging between his lead units as C Company pressed on, at 1100 hours Lt Col Mildren decided to commit his reserve. When B/38th surged forward the Germans panicked and fled, abandoning numerous weapons. Tanks also advanced on 1/38th's right, assisting the infantry in the area between Dodge and Ford Woods. By 1330 hours B Company was clearing the smoking remains of the western part of Ford Woods, joined by C Company. A Company followed up, and by dusk the battalion was dug in along the southern fringe of the woods, overlooking the D972. 1/38th's losses on 11 July were 13 killed and 52 wounded.

The paratroops on Hill 192 fought determinedly, but were overwhelmed by the power and skill of the US assault. Here, a paratrooper fires an MG 42, the standard section machine gun around which German defences were so often built. (BA 1011-579-1957-26)

Stand C6: St-Georges-d'Elle

DIRECTIONS: Continue along the D95 towards St-Georges-d'Elle. After about 500 metres you will reach another sharp bend in the road; this marked the boundary between 38th and 23rd Infantry Regiments. Carry on for 1 km into the village, pausing to look south for clear views into the western part of Purple Heart Draw (*see Stand C7*). In 1944 St-Georges was the scene of intense patrol activity, and the village changed hands on several occasions from mid-June onwards. On 11 July, however, all but the southern-most houses were held by the Americans.

The section of road you have just walked along was the line of departure for Lt Col John Hightower's 1/23rd Infantry, supported by C/741st Tank Battalion. Its objective lay on the D972, protecting 38th Infantry Regiment's left flank near the village of la Croix Rouge. Opposition here came mainly from elements of III/9th Paratroop Regiment, holding the southern side of Purple Heart Draw. This steep-sided gully, which had been sown with anti-personnel mines, ran parallel with 1/23rd's line of departure barely 200 metres from it. East of the D195, the defenders were from I/5th Paratroop Regiment.

THE ACTION: 1/23rd Infantry began its attack at 0600 hours from a position 270 metres behind the line of departure, at the rear of the 'safety zone' from which all troops withdrew during the preliminary bombardment. C Company was on the right, west of the D390 road junction, with A Company on the left. Initial progress was good, and no significant resistance was met until US troops reached Purple Heart Draw.

Simultaneously L/23rd Infantry, from the regiment's 3rd Battalion, launched a separate attack in the eastern part of St-Georges-d'Elle. The aim was to pin German troops in this area, to prevent them interfering with the assault on Hill 192. Because of this, the objective was limited to only a field or two south of the D95. At the cost of 3 killed and 20 wounded, the objective was achieved, and L/23rd dug in to consolidate.

Stand C7: Purple Heart Draw

DIRECTIONS: From St-Georges church, head south on the D195, signposted 'Vers [towards] D972'. After about 150 metres you will enter Purple Heart Draw, now heavily overgrown west of the road. Continue to the bottom, where in 1944 there were several farm buildings and a small bridge (no longer present) across the dry stream bed. These features were held by German paratroops, who could deliver enfilading fire against anyone trying to cross the draw from the north.

THE ACTION: After crossing the D95, A/23rd met strong resistance at Purple Heart Draw. Despite covering fire from four Shermans which lined up north of the gully, when 1st Platoon launched a frontal attack it ran into heavy artillery, mortar and

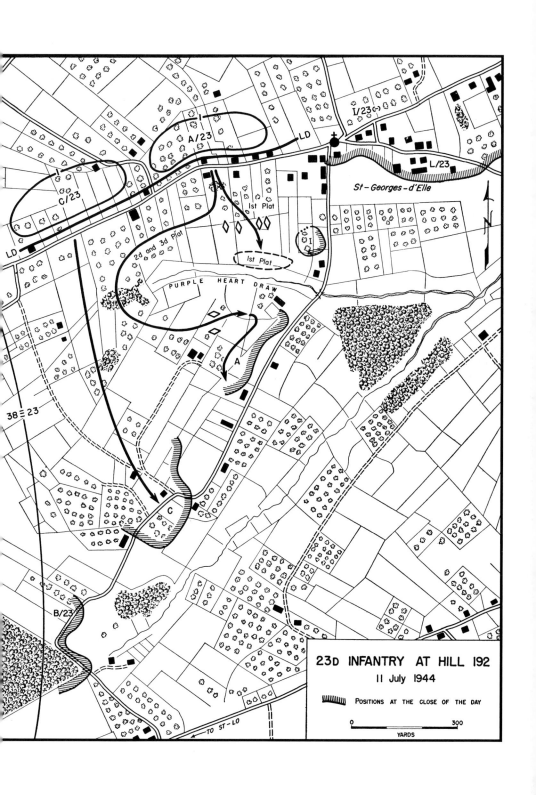

LD

A/23

LD

C/23

L/23

St–Georges–d'Elle

1st Plat

2d and 3d Plat

1st Plat

I

LD

PURPLE HEART DRAW

A

38 ≡ 23

C

B/23

TO ST-LO

23D INFANTRY AT HILL 192

11 July 1944

POSITIONS AT THE CLOSE OF THE DAY

0   300

YARDS

N

machine-gun fire from the south and east. This caused many casualties and the advance ground to a halt. An attempt to outflank the draw to the west by 2nd Platoon also ran into trouble. However, two Shermans from C/741st reinforced the outflanking move, pushing along the south side of the gully to within 30 metres of the defended buildings near the D195 bridge. The tanks then used high explosive shells to destroy these structures. 3rd Platoon also moved round the head of the draw to mop up resistance, and by midday was joined by the rest of the company. Later a platoon of I Company (3rd Battalion) advanced south along the D195, losing 7 killed and 25 wounded before halting near the bridge. At 1700 hours elements of 2/23rd Infantry came up from reserve, relieving A Company on 1/23rd's left flank.

Some of the best views of Purple Heart Draw are from the D95 west of St-Georges-d'Elle. This view, looking south, shows the western end of the draw, around which elements of I/23rd Infantry moved to outflank the German defences further east. *(ST)*

Stand C8: la Baroterie

DIRECTIONS: Continue for 700 metres, passing la Blanchetière on your right, to la Baroterie. From here you can look back north along the route taken by 1/23rd. The view to the north-east towards the Forêt de Cerisy is impressive and panoramic.

THE ACTION: While A/23rd Infantry struggled to cross Purple Heart Draw, C Company was opposed by only a few machine-gun nests, which were eliminated by rifle-grenades. The most significant problems occurred when contact was temporarily lost with 1/38th Infantry, on C Company's right. However, although this slowed the latter's advance, once liaison was re-established the attack gathered momentum. C/23rd approached la Baroterie, where a Panzer IV was lying in wait. According to US accounts, an unknown infantryman crept up along a hedgerow, dropped two grenades through the turret hatches and knocked out the tank. C/23rd ended the day only a few hundred metres from its objective, dug in around the buildings of la Baroterie.

Unsurprisingly, relatively few prisoners were taken during the attack on Hill 192. This wounded paratrooper, supported by two grim-faced Americans, is one of them. *(IWM AP29650)*

Stand C9: le Village aux Moines

DIRECTIONS: Continue south for a few hundred metres to a small cluster of buildings to the right of the road, close to the eastern end of the Bois du Soulaire. A little further on, from the left-hand side you can look south-east to see the D972 and beyond.

THE ACTION: During the afternoon of 11 July, B/23rd Infantry, 1st Battalion's reserve company, moved forward to this position, covering the gap between 1/38th on the right and C/23rd on the left.

> **The US success on 11 July was characterised by very considerable bravery and resourcefulness:**
>
> 'Five months after the attack, the tankers [of C/741st Tank Battalion] still spoke with wonder about one 200-lb engineer, Sergeant Doras Goodyear, who not only directed the overall operation of his demolition squads but ran from tank to tank to wipe off periscopes with his handkerchief when they became clouded with the early-morning dew. Goodyear was a tower of strength all day, riding the tanks to communicate when the EE8 telephones [telephones mounted on the rear of each Sherman, which facilitated communication with the tank crew] did not click, picking out locations and directing the tank drivers, and guiding the tanks to new locations if enemy fire started to get too heavy; his reward for the day's action was a Silver Star.'
>
> *Source:* 2nd Infantry Division combat interviews, RG 407, Box 24014, Folder 12, USNA.

ENDING THE TOUR: To return to St-Lô, continue a few hundred metres south to the D972 and turn right.

TOUR D

29TH INFANTRY DIVISION'S ASSAULT ON ST-LÔ

OBJECTIVE: This tour examines 29th Infantry Division's attempts to capture St-Lô between 11 and 18 July.

DURATION/SUITABILITY: This tour lasts half a day. The total distance from St-Lô to Stand D7 is 15 km, generally along quiet roads; the tour is therefore suitable for cyclists. For those with mobility difficulties all stands are accessible by car, although Stand D6 should be approached from the D972, not the route described below.

Stand D1: Belle Fontaine

DIRECTIONS: Leave St-Lô on the D6 and turn right after 3 km onto the D95, signposted to la Luzerne. This road marked the approximate position of 3rd Paratroop Division's front line after the US offensive stalled in mid-June. On 29 June elements of 3rd Armored Division advanced almost to la Luzerne (*see p. 63*), but were repulsed and fell back to the D448. On Tuesday 11 July German positions in this area were held by II/9th Paratroop Regiment, facing 115th Infantry Regiment to the north. Troops of Battlegroup *Böhm* were also in the area, astride the D6.

Belle Fontaine, looking north up the draw used by 5/9th Paratroop Regiment to infiltrate the US front early on 11 July. (ST)

Head south-east along the D95. Park by the reservoir in la Luzerne and walk 100 metres uphill, ascending the bank or looking through the gate on your right for fine views of the

US positions 2400 hrs 11 July

1 2/115th Infantry
2 3/115th Infantry
3 1/115th Infantry
4 2/116th Infantry
5 1/116th Infantry
6 3/116th Infantry
7 2/175th Infantry
8 2/38th Infantry

a St-Lô Cemetery

Base maps:
IGN 1312E, IGN 1313E,
IGN 1412OT, IGN1413O

POINT 101
(1944 maps)

0   1   2

Martinville Ridge to the south. Then continue to Belle Fontaine, about 1 km away. Pull over and look up and down the valley on both sides of the road. This was the route used by elements of II/9th Paratroop Regiment during their raid on 1/115th Infantry Regiment on 11 July.

THE ACTION: At 0130 hours on 11 July (*as described on p. 84*) German paratroops attacked the positions held by 1/115th Infantry about 1 km north-east of this stand, in the Bretel–Hôtel Dufayel area. The attackers were led by *Oberleutnant* (First Lieutenant) Werner Kersting, commander of 5/9th Paratroop Regiment; estimates of the raiders' strength vary from 200 to 400 men. The attack's purpose is unclear, although it may simply have been to maintain an aggressive spirit at a time when the Germans had been on the defensive for exactly a month.

Following the paratroops' retreat, at midday on 11 July 1/115th launched its own assault in accordance with 29th Division's overall plan. But the understrength American companies (at about 100 men, they were barely half their normal size) made little progress against determined opposition, and had to dig in north of Belle Fontaine. Attempts by 3/115th to push south to la Luzerne were even less successful, and were stopped barely 100 metres beyond the line of departure.

The Americans tried again the next day, hampered by artillery and minefields, though not by German troops, who had withdrawn overnight. 1/115th cleared Belle Fontaine and then extended its front towards la Luzerne. Here it joined up with 3/115th, which had already occupied part of the village. Further movement south ran into small-arms and mortar fire from the Martinville Ridge, and the US troops halted on the slopes north of the Rau de la Dollée stream. West of the D6, 2/115th Infantry also had a disappointing day, being counter-attacked at le Bourg d'Enfer and driven back to its former positions. In total, 115th Regiment lost 21 killed and 87 wounded on 12 July, for no significant gain.

Heavy fighting continued in this area on 13 July, particularly west of the D6 near le Bourg d'Enfer, but 115th Regiment suffered over 100 casualties and advanced only a few hedgerows. After a day of rest and re-organisation, at 0600 hours on 15 July the Americans moved forward again. 1/115th led the attack immediately east of the D6, with two platoons of Shermans (from 747th Tank Battalion) assisting.

The Martinville Ridge as seen from la Luzerne, with the approximate location of Stand D3 in the centre. *(ST)*

Colonel Godwin Ordway, commanding 115th Infantry Regiment, described the action:

'The [1st] battalion was held up by fire from Germans west of the road, also by fire from 35th Division on its right rear. The 35th Division's artillery stopped as soon as CO telephoned, but [Ordway] had "a hell of a time" stopping the small arms fire. To break the jam, he had to commit the 2nd Battalion through the 3rd Battalion. The 2nd Battalion was stopped by fire from Conchais [*sic* – le Cauchais] and from the north slope of the Martinville Ridge… The 2nd Battalion stopped approximately abreast and east of the 1st Battalion. The 3rd Battalion was not committed.'

Source: 29th Infantry Division combat interviews, RG 407, Box 24034, Folder 83, USNA.

On 16 July, 2/115th was ordered to advance to relieve elements of 116th Regiment south of the Martinville Ridge, but once again

could not get across the Rau de la Dollée. Further details of 115th Regiment's role in the battle on 17–18 July are given at Stand D7.

Stand D2: St-André-de-l'Épine cemetery

DIRECTIONS: Continue along the D95 for 1.75 km. This area was occupied during the battle by elements of 29th Reconnaissance Troop, covering the gap between 115th and 116th Infantry Regiments. Park by the green gates of the cemetery on the western edge of St-André-de-l'Épine. From its north-east corner you can survey the ground over which the Americans attacked on 11 July, pushing back elements of II/ and III/9th Paratroop Regiment and outflanking the devastated village to the east.

THE ACTION: The US attack began at 0600 hours on 11 July, led by Major Sidney V. Bingham's 2/116th Infantry, assisted by B/121st Engineer Combat Battalion and A/747th Tank Battalion. The US troops were formed into assault teams, each comprising an infantry squad, one tank and four engineers. Each group was allocated an attack frontage of one field.

The tactics used by the assault teams were based on 29th Division's earlier experiences in the *bocage*. As soon as the team was in position along a hedgerow, the tank would fire white phosphorous rounds into the field corners opposite to neutralise German heavy weapons, and sweep the 'enemy' hedgerow with its machine guns. The infantry then advanced, avoiding the flanking hedges – where the Germans had fixed lines of fire – and using fire and movement tactics to attack the enemy positions. Their assault was also covered by smoke bombs from their own 60-mm mortar. Simultaneously, the engineers made a gap in the first hedgerow. To do this, each Sherman was fitted with two metal prongs, welded to the front of the vehicle. These were used to gouge holes in the hedgerow base, into which explosive charges were placed and detonated. The tank and mortar team could then move through the gap to the next hedgerow, where the process would begin again.

The view north from St-André-de-l'Épine cemetery. 116th Infantry Regiment attacked through the fields on the right, moving in the general direction of the camera position. *(Author)*

Using these tactics, 2/116th attacked with two companies forward, E west of the D59 and F to the east; G Company was in reserve. The Germans offered determined opposition, and the Americans suffered heavy casualties as they pushed south. However, although by 1100 hours 2/116th's rifle companies were down to 60 effectives apiece, at this point German resistance cracked. Bingham's men then advanced quickly through fields littered with German corpses, victims of the supporting artillery bombardment.

By early afternoon they reached the junction with the D195 south of St-André-de-l'Épine, and turned right onto the Martinville Ridge. At this point the battalion was about 6 km north-east of St-Lô, and making steady progress towards Objective A, which lay astride the D195 north of le Mesnil Sigard de Haut.

A view south from the Martinville Ridge, taken from the approximate positions held by 1/116th Infantry late on 11 July. *(ST)*

At about 1300 hours Colonel Charles Canham, commanding the 116th, ordered the rest of his regiment forward. Lt Col Lawrence Meeks' 3/116th moved first, advancing south towards Objective B, on the D972 at la Boulaye. Major Thomas Dallas' 1/116th followed, tasked to pass between the other battalions after Objectives A and B were seized, and press on to la Madeleine, 1 km east of St-Lô. Later on 11 July Lt Col Millard Bowen's 2/175th Infantry Regiment also headed south, digging in beside the D59 to protect 116th Regiment's rear as it advanced towards St-Lô.

Stand D3: The water tower crossroads

DIRECTIONS: Continue through the rebuilt village of St-André-de-l'Épine and turn right onto the D59. You are now following the axis of 116th Infantry Regiment's advance on 11 July. On the left-hand side is Hill 192, visited during Tour C. Drive south for 500 metres and turn right onto the D195, which runs along the crest of the Martinville Ridge. After about 1.5 km you will pass the positions occupied by 1/116th late on 11 July. 750 metres beyond that, you will come to 2/116th's front line on the 11th. Continue for another 500 metres and pull over before the crossroads, with a water tower to your front left. From the area of the crossroads you have good views of the high ground both north and south.

The road junction at Stand D3, looking north. The cross-section through the hedgerow bank gives an indication of the difficulties met by US troops as they tried to break their way through such obstacles during the battle for St-Lô. *(ST)*

THE ACTION: Despite Maj Gen Gerhardt's exhortations to push on to St-Lô, by nightfall on 11 July the exhausted soldiers of 2/116th had halted about 1.5 km east of Martinville. Meanwhile, 3rd Paratroop Division worked frantically to build a new front north-east of St-Lô. To do this, the division's engineer battalion was brought into the line, where it reinforced the survivors of 9th Paratroop Regiment. Several assault guns from II Paratroop Corps' *Sturmgeschütz* Brigade also arrived, although requests for further reinforcements from Seventh Army were refused by its commander, *SS-Oberstgruppenführer* Hausser.

On the morning of 12 July the Americans renewed their attack along the Martinville Ridge and the D972. German troops south of the highway between St-Pierre-de-Semilly and la Barre-de-Semilly (on 'Hill 101') were well placed to observe their movement, and rained down artillery and mortar fire. This slowed the US assault to a crawl, and by nightfall Bingham's battalion had advanced only a few hundred metres, roughly to where you are now standing. Although 2/175th joined the attack in the early evening, it also found it difficult to get forward, and halted on Bingham's right. Meanwhile, east of la Boulaye, 3/116th fought all day to consolidate its positions on the D972, assisted by Lt Col Edward Gill's 3/175th. Gerhardt urged his commanders forward, but they could do little in the face of the German firepower. The Germans also used ruses to disrupt the advance, breaking into 747th Tank Battalion's radio net and ordering its Shermans to report back to the regimental command post. The tankmen did as instructed, leaving the infantry temporarily without armoured support.

Stand D4: le Mesnil Sigard de Bas

DIRECTIONS: Turn left at the crossroads and drive downhill to the quiet road junction 250 metres beyond le Mesnil Sigard de Bas.

THE ACTION: On the morning of 12 July 1/116th moved forward, cutting downhill into the valley of the Rau de la Pièrie towards la Madeleine. The battalion advanced in column of companies, reaching a point near this stand after some bitter fighting. Three German tanks and two self-propelled guns then attacked along the draw from the west, blasting the hedgerows and causing heavy casualties. A concentration of American 105-mm shells and bazookas destroyed two of the tanks, but the self-propelled guns carried on moving and shooting for some time. Nevertheless, the battalion held its ground and by nightfall was dug in, ready to continue the assault the next day.

Stand D5: Martinville

DIRECTIONS: Return to the water tower crossroads and continue west on the D195 for 1 km, parking on the verge on the right hand side of the road at the hamlet of Martinville.

THE ACTION: On 13 July the Americans continued their push west, fiercely opposed by the Germans. This time the main effort was made by Colonel Ollie Reed's 175th Infantry, attacking along the D972. However, poor weather caused a planned air strike to be cancelled, and shortages of fuel and ammunition

BATTLEFIELD TOURS

delayed the supporting tanks. Partly as a result, 175th Infantry Regiment made little progress. Later in the day 2/116th renewed its attack along the D195, but advanced only a short distance. In the evening the Germans brought up II/8th Paratroop Regiment, which was still relatively fresh, and used it to relieve the remnants of 9th Paratroop Regiment. Gerhardt also decided to use 14 July to re-organize his forces and bring up replacements. On the night of 13/14 July 2/116th therefore pulled back to St-André-de-l'Épine. Its positions were occupied by 1/116th, which handed over its own area of responsibility to 3/175th Infantry. 3/116th also moved back to the Martinville Ridge, leaving 2/175th astride the D972 north-west of St-Pierre-de-Semilly. Simultaneously, Colonel Canham departed to take up a senior appointment in 8th Infantry Division; his successor as commander of 116th Infantry Regiment was Colonel Philip R. Dwyer.

The view north from Martinville, showing the area across which 115th Infantry Regiment tried unsuccessfully to advance between 11 and 16 July. (ST)

At 0515 hours on 15 July, 29th Division attacked again. No significant effort was made along the D972, owing to the continued German observation over the road from Hill 101, further south. Instead, the principal blow took place along the D195, supported by a renewed attack by 115th Infantry Regiment from la Luzerne. 3/116th Infantry, now commanded by Major Thomas D. Howie, led the assault, supported by a company of Shermans, a platoon of Stuart light tanks from 747th Tank Battalion and some engineers.

Howie's troops pressed hard throughout the morning of 15 July, but suffered considerable losses to German artillery, which knocked out seven tanks. During the afternoon I Company tried to outflank Martinville from the north, but was stopped 750 metres short. 1/116th moved forward in support, but gained only one hedgerow. The Americans regrouped, and tried again at 1930 hours. This time they attacked on both sides of the D195, Major Bingham's 2nd Battalion north of the road and Major Dallas' 1st Battalion to the south. Despite strong artillery support and strikes by a dozen P-47 Thunderbolts, little progress was made. Observing – rather unfairly – that his troops had not 'made the grade', Gerhardt decided to halt the attack, and ordered his forces to dig in for the night.

Unknown to Gerhardt, however, 3rd Paratroop Engineer Battalion's line had finally ruptured. Led by F Company, 2/116th swept through the German positions north-east of Martinville during the evening. G Company cleared the hamlet, while E and F Companies moved south, heading for la Madeleine through the steep-sided valley south of Martinville. At this point Major Bingham, who had been checking on his rear elements, received the order to stop and consolidate. However, after following the telephone wires laid by his men as they advanced, he found most of his battalion already astride the D972. Bingham decided to establish a perimeter defence and await reinforcement. Soon after, the telephone line linking him to his battalion staff near Martinville was broken, although Bingham could still communicate sporadically with 116th Regiment's headquarters by radio. German troops then moved forward again, isolating 2/116th from the rest of the regiment on the Martinville Ridge.

In accordance with Gerhardt's orders, 1/116th dug in about 500 metres east of Martinville, together with half of G Company, some of 2/116th's heavy weapons and all of Bingham's headquarters personnel. The next day the battalion was heavily counter-attacked by the Germans, supported by artillery and at least three tanks.

A Company, holding 1/116th's right flank immediately south of the D195, had no surviving officers and was commanded on 16 July by Private Harold E. Peterson:

'The results of the [German] tank fire were deadly. Raking the hedgerow from one end to the other, it blew out great gaps and killed or wounded men with every shot. The bazooka team was killed... The entire right flank of

Company A was buckling and beginning to fall back before the deadly tank fire and the rest of the line melted with them. Peterson retreated with them, he and Sergeant Thomas Fried dragging a wounded man along with them "like a sled". The Company recoiled back on the hedgerow behind them where the Battalion CP [Command Post] was located... A captain at the Battalion CP... ordered the men back to their line. To Peterson that meant certain death, but the officer insisted. Leaving the wounded man... at the Battalion CP... Peterson managed to rally the company. But instead of taking up their former position, which he regarded as untenable, Peterson took a rifle equipped with a grenade launcher and some rifle-grenades and sneaked up the left hedgerow into the field ahead where he was able to obtain a field of fire upon the enemy tank. Then he opened fire. He registered six direct hits on the tank with rifle-grenades and the tank pulled out in retreat.'

Source: 29th Infantry Division combat interviews, RG 407, Box 24034, Folder 83, USNA.

Looking west along 116th Infantry Regiment's axis of advance towards St-Lô, from a position about 750 metres east of Martinville. This area was the scene of the violent German attacks on 16 July, which were only just held. *(ST)*

Thanks to the gallantry of Peterson and men like him, 1/116th held its positions throughout 16 July, although the Americans were unable to advance any further along the Martinville Ridge or restore connections with Bingham's force to the south.

Stand D6: la Heuperie

DIRECTIONS: Leaving your vehicle at Martinville, walk down the track south of the road into the valley of the Rau de la Pièrie (*photo below*). Go past the white-painted gate on your left to a point where the path bends hard right. Look through the gate here to the modern buildings on the slope beyond. To proceed to the valley bottom, take the steep gully track on your left, which joins a surfaced road about 200 metres further down. If you wish to do so, continue uphill to 2/116th's position astride the D972. Bear in mind that this area has changed greatly since 1944 (there is now a commercial zone where once there was *bocage*), and it is therefore difficult to visualise the action when you arrive. Nevertheless, you can get an excellent sense of how the US troops were able to infiltrate south from the evening of 15 July onwards by following the route described. The silence at the bottom of the valley, only a short distance from the bustle of modern St-Lô, is striking.

A view south at Martinville, showing the track to Stand D6 (to the right of the house). *(ST)*

THE ACTION: Bingham's 200 or so men spent 16 July under sporadic mortar and artillery fire. However, the Germans launched no significant counter-attacks, and largely ignored 2/116th's presence behind their lines. The main source of discomfort for the GIs was a shortage of food and water, although this problem was partly remedied when two wells were discovered nearby.

Gerhardt was now aware of Bingham's isolation, and anxious to provide relief. He also believed the Germans were about to break, and ordered his entire division to resume the offensive on 17 July. Late on 16 July, 116th Regiment received 270 replacements, together with instructions to secure Martinville and the routes heading south-west. Once again Major Howie's 3/116th was given the lead role. It was ordered to move south, join up with 2/116th, and then attack west into St-Lô. Further north, 115th Infantry Regiment would strike south from la Luzerne, while 175th Infantry was to renew its assault along the D972.

Access to la Heuperie requires a descent down the steep gully to the left of the gate. This track was almost certainly used by US troops between 15 and 18 July. (ST)

Early on 17 July a group of about 60 soldiers, mostly from G/116th (attached to 1/116th) infiltrated through the hedges north of the D195 and reached Martinville, which was found to be unoccupied. Assisted by a tank destroyer and an anti-tank gun, they secured the village, set up roadblocks and established a string of positions back along the ridge to 1/116th's front line. Meanwhile, at 0430 hours 3/116th began its own attack to the south-west. On

Major Howie's orders, the assault was conducted stealthily, with the troops under instructions to use bayonets and grenades, but to open fire only in an emergency. The Americans were also shrouded by an early morning mist, and benefited from a fortuitous decision to attack on the boundary between two German companies.

Howie's men made excellent progress, and at 0600 hours reached the D972 a few hundred metres west of Bingham's position. Contact was established with 2/116th, rations shared, and preparations made to continue the attack. German supply vehicles travelling northwards to la Planche du Bois were also engaged. At 0730 hours Colonel Dwyer telephoned, ordering Howie to push on to St-Lô. Soon afterwards, however, 3/116th's command post was hit by mortar fire and Howie was killed. This caused much disruption, and marked the beginning of an intense German bombardment, which continued both here and on the Martinville Ridge for several hours. Howie's successor, Captain William Puntenney, therefore decided to form a perimeter defence, and to await further developments.

At about 1800 hours the Germans counter-attacked 3/116th's position from the south, but were driven back. Later, however, tanks were heard assembling near la Roque. Puntenney's men had only a single bazooka round left, but their radios were still working, so artillery assistance and an air strike were called for. These requests were approved by XIX Corps, and after instructing 3/116th to lay out recognition panels and use its soldiers' red undershirts to indicate their positions, 506th Fighter Squadron was briefed in the air. Shortly after 2100 hours, it attacked.

Captain Puntenney described the effects of the air strike:

'[The air attack] came very quickly, with the bombs falling close to our lines. The morale effect on our troops was electric. Discouragement disappeared and the confidence of the early morning was re-established. The bombing had an equally potent effect on the enemy's morale, leaving them demoralized or ineffective. Many Germans came running into our lines for protection.'

Source: 29th Infantry Division combat interviews, RG 407, Box 24034, Folder 83, USNA.

As a result of this support, 2/116th and 3/116th were able to maintain their positions astride the D972. By now, however, they

GIs advance towards St-Lô past a burned out US half-track mounting quad .50-calibre machine guns. This may be the vehicle destroyed during the abortive attempt to send aid to 2/ and 3/116th Infantry on 17 July. *(USNA)*

were very short of supplies. Although artillery spotter aircraft dropped blood plasma on 17 July, and a captured Austrian doctor provided medical assistance, several wounded men died. During the afternoon of the 17th the Americans tried to send a convoy from the Martinville Ridge to la Madeleine, using two half-tracks mounting quad .50-calibre anti-aircraft cannon to blast a path through German resistance. But all the routes south from the D195 were blocked by debris, and the attempt was abandoned when one of the half-tracks was destroyed west of Martinville. Later that night, however, 40 volunteers from the 116th's Anti-Tank and Cannon Companies managed to infiltrate cross-country to 2/116th, carrying essential supplies. Together with material taken from a captured German ammunition dump, this allowed the forward troops to hold their positions overnight.

At 1045 hours on 18 July another effort was made to open a corridor to la Madeleine. This involved Captain James Rabbitt's A Company (1/116th), which plunged into the valley of the Rau de la Pièrie from Martinville, leaving small parties in each field as it advanced towards the positions held by the isolated battalions. This time the attempt succeeded. By midday a link-up was achieved with 2/116th and 3/116th, and the corridor reinforced. Wounded were then evacuated to the Martinville Ridge, while supplies flowed in the opposite direction. By this point little resistance was encountered from the Germans, who seemed confused and inclined to withdraw. Some fighting still took place, however, notably when a 'sizeable' group of Germans marched in column along the draw and were cut down by US machine guns.

On the evening of 18 July 116th Regiment received news that Task Force *Cota* had entered St-Lô. Consequently, although patrols reconnoitred towards the town, Bingham's and Puntenney's men remained where they were. On 19 July they were relieved by 2/115th Infantry. The next day, 35th Infantry Division assumed formal responsibility for the entire sector, and the rest of 29th Division withdrew for a well-earned rest. A week later it was to re-enter the battle, this time as part of the exploitation force for the American break-through offensive, Operation 'Cobra'.

Stand D7: la Planche du Bois

DIRECTIONS: Return to Martinville and continue south-west on the D195, which descends steeply to la Planche du Bois. Turn right onto the D88 and pull over beyond the bridge, looking back in the direction from which you have just come.

THE ACTION: Following the disappointments of 11–16 July, 115th Infantry Regiment attacked again on the 17th. 1st and 3rd Battalions – both badly understrength – advanced south-west towards St-Lô, east of the D6, but met heavy opposition near le Cauchais and made limited progress. Hoping to find another way forward, Gerhardt ordered Colonel Ordway to send 2/115th south-east to the Martinville Ridge. From here the battalion would head west, outflanking German resistance at le Cauchais. The objective was the hamlet of la Planche du Bois, at the junction of the Rau de la Dollée and the Rau de la Pièrie valleys.

2/115th, now commanded by Major Asbury Jackson, moved

forward during the afternoon. Few German troops were encountered, and by 1600 hours the battalion was just north of Martinville. However, on reaching the ridge, its weapons company was hit by an intense mortar concentration, and suffered numerous casualties. German snipers were also encountered in Martinville, which had to be cleared again. When Ordway visited 2/115th after nightfall, he found it digging in. He insisted that the advance be resumed, and at midnight Jackson's men set off, reaching la Planche du Bois soon afterwards. Later on 18 July 2/115th pushed further south-west towards the outskirts of St-Lô. As German resistance collapsed, 3/115th also headed south. Meanwhile, 1/115th joined Task Force *Cota* for the final assault into St-Lô (*see pp. 111–2*).

View from the gate shown in the photo on p. 180, looking across the roofs of la Heuperie (in the valley bottom) to the modern commercial buildings at la Madeleine, held by 3/116th Infantry on 17–18 July. (ST)

ENDING THE TOUR: From la Planche du Bois, head uphill along the D88 and turn left onto the D6. From here you are following the route taken by Task Force *Cota* as it advanced into St-Lô on the afternoon of 18 July. Follow this road to the D972, passing the town cemetery – where 1/115th's command post was established on 19 July – on your left. Follow signs to 'Centre Ville' to reach the Place Charles de Gaulle at the heart of St-Lô.

PART FOUR

ON YOUR
RETURN

FURTHER RESEARCH

There are many sources of additional information available on the battle. Some suggestions on worthwhile books are given below. The most valuable primary sources used in the preparation of this study, however, were the documents and photographs held at the US National Archives and Records Administration at College Park, a few miles from the centre of Washington DC. In addition to unit war diaries, this archive contains some astonishingly detailed after-action reports and combat interviews, some of which are quoted in this study.

DOCUMENTS

Among the most useful were (all in Record Group 407):

2nd Infantry Division, Hill 192, 11–12 July 1944, Box 24014, Folder 12; 3rd US Armored Division, Villiers-Fossard, 29 June – 11 July 1944, Box 24088, Folder 259; 29th Infantry Division, Omaha Beach, 6–11 June, Box 24014, Folder 81(i); 29th Infantry Division, June–July 1944, Box 24014, Folder 81(ii); 29th Infantry Division, Battle for St. Lo, 11–18 July 1944, Box 24034, Folder 83; 30th Infantry Division, Normandy, 15 June – 11 July 1944, Box 24037, Folder 94; 35th Infantry Division, Normandy, 12–31 July 1944, Box 24042, Folder 106; 899th Tank Destroyer Battalion, 11 July 1944, Box 24205, Folder 1055.

A number of translated German records were located at the same source. The most important were: Seventh Army War Diary, 6 June – 15 August 1944, Box 24154, Folder 488; Seventh Army Telephone Log, 6 June – 15 August 1944, Box 24154, Folder 487; Narrative of the Operations of 352nd Infantry Division 7 June – 18 July 1944, by Fritz Ziegelmann (Manuscripts B-241; 433; 434; 435; 436; 437; 438; 439; 455); Operations of the 3rd Paratroop Division during the Invasion of France, June–August 1944, by Richard Schimpf (Manuscript B-541).

SECONDARY SOURCES

Allsup, John S., *Hedgerow Hell*, Editions Heimdal, Bayeux, 1985.
Badsey, Stephen, *Utah Beach*, Sutton Publishing, Stroud, 2004.
Badsey, Stephen & Bean, Tim, *Omaha Beach*, Sutton Publishing, Stroud, 2004.

Above: Ingenuity in the field. Engineers operate a washing machine improvised from captured German equipment, near St-Lô, 17 July. *(USNA)*

Page 185: Private Robert Vance, a US motorcycle dispatch rider, photographed near St-Jean-de-Daye. Dispatch riders performed a valuable role in maintaining communications during the battle for St-Lô. *(USNA)*

Balkoski, Joseph, *Beyond the Beachhead: The 29th Infantry Division in Normandy*, Stackpole Books, Mechanicsburg, 1989.

Binkoski, Joseph & Plaut, Arthur, *The 115th Infantry Regiment in World War II*, The Battery Press, Nashville, 1988.

Blumenson, Martin, *U.S. Army in World War II, European Theatre of Operations: Breakout and Pursuit*, Office of the Chief of Military History, Washington DC, 1961.

Bradley, Omar N., *A Soldier's Story*, Henry Holt & Company, New York, 1951.

Cawthon, Charles R., *Other Clay; a Remembrance of the World War II Infantry*, University of Nebraska Press, Lincoln 2004.

Doubler, Michael D., *Busting the Bocage: American Combined Operations in France, 6 June – 31 July 1944*, Combat Studies Institute, Fort Leavenworth, 1988.

Doubler, Michael D., *Closing with the Enemy: How GIs fought the war in Europe*, University Press of Kansas, Lawrence, 1994.

Ewing, Joseph H., *29 Let's Go! A History of the 29th Infantry Division in World War II*, Infantry Journal Press, Washington DC, 1948.

Gordon, Harold J. (ed. Gordon, Nancy M.), *One Man's War; a Memoir of World War II*, The Apex Press, New York, 1999.

ON YOUR RETURN

Harrison, Gordon A., *U.S. Army in World War II, European Theatre of Operations: Cross-Channel Attack*, Office of the Chief of Military History, Washington DC, 1984 edition.

Hewitt, Robert L., *Work Horse of the Western Front: The Story of the 30th Infantry Division*, Infantry Journal Press, Washington DC, 1946.

Hinsley, F. H. *et al.*, *British Intelligence in the Second World War*, Volume 3, Part II, Her Majesty's Stationery Office, London, 1988.

Historical Division, US War Department, *Omaha Beachhead (6 June – 13 June 1944)*, Center of Military History, Washington DC, 1984 edition.

Historical Division, US War Department, *Utah Beach to Cherbourg (6 June – 27 June 1944)*, Center of Military History, Washington DC, 1984 edition.

Historical Division, US War Department, *St-Lô (7 July – 19 July 1944)*, Center of Military History, Washington DC, 1984 edition.

Huston, James A., *Biography of a Battalion; the Life and Times of an Infantry Battalion in Europe in World War II*, Stackpole Books, Mechanicsburg, 2003 edition.

Isby, David C. (Ed.), *Fighting in Normandy: The German Army from D-Day to Villers-Bocage*, Greenhill Books, London, 2001.

Johns, Glover S., *The Clay Pigeons of St. Lô*, Stackpole Books, Mechanicsburg, 2002 edition.

Ritgen, Helmut, *Die Geschichte der Panzer Lehr Division im Westen 1944–1945*, Motorbuch Verlag, Stuttgart, 1979.

Reynolds, Michael, *Eagles and Bulldogs in Normandy 1944*, Spellmount Ltd., Staplehurst, 2003.

Weigley, Russell, *Eisenhower's Lieutenants*, Indiana University Press, Bloomington, 1981.

Zetterling, Niklas, *Normandy 1944: German Military Organization, Combat Power and Organizational Effectiveness*, J. J. Fedorowicz Publishing Inc., Winnipeg, 2000.

Useful Addresses

Imperial War Museum, Lambeth Road, London SE1 6HZ; tel: 020 7416 5320; email: <mail@iwm.org.uk>; web: <www.iwm.org.uk>.

UK National Archives, Public Record Office, Kew, Richmond, Surrey TW9 4DU; tel: 020 8876 3444; email: <enquiry@nationalarchives.gov.uk>; web: <www.nationalarchives.gov.uk>.

US National Archives, The National Archives and Records Administration, 8601 Adelphi Road, College Park, MD 20740–6001; tel: +01 866 272 6272; web: <www.archives.gov>.

ON YOUR RETURN

INDEX

Page numbers in *italics* denote an illustration.